Pie Style

Harvest Time Concord Grape Pie (page 74)

Pie Style

Stunning Designs *and* Flavorful Fillings
You Can Make at Home

Helen Nugent

Founder of Pie-Eyed Girl

Photography by James Brand

PAGE STREET
PUBLISHING CO.

First published in 2020 by
Page Street Publishing Co.
27 Congress Street, Suite 105
Salem, MA 01970
www.pagestreetpublishing.com

Distributed by Macmillan, sales in Canada by The Canadian Manda Group.

24   23   22   21   20   2   3   4   5   6

ISBN-13: 978-1-64567-077-3
ISBN-10: 1-64567-077-5

Library of Congress Control Number: 2019957239

Cover and book design by Kylie Alexander for Page Street Publishing Co.
Photography by James Brand

Printed and bound in the United States

To Stephen and Maeve,
who taught me anything is possible.

To Jim, Devlin and Liam
for making everything possible.

Table *of* Contents

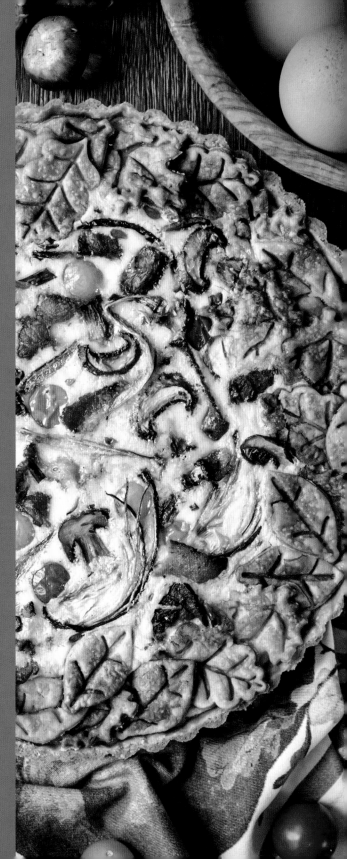

Introduction

One of the questions I'm asked most often is how I learned to bake and decorate pies. The quick and easy answer is, I learned from my mother. But it's a bit more complicated than that.

My mother was a 1970s stay-at-home mom who raised five daughters while my father worked long hours at the local hospital as a doctor. That meant that while we were at school, she had time for things like baking. And she was good at it. So good, in fact, that she refused to allow anything that "came out of a package" (as she liked to say) come through our front door. And while my sisters and I could occasionally cajole her into a family trip to a fast-food restaurant, never—and I do mean never—was the rule relaxed for baked goods. So, while my friends were throwing another pop tart in the toaster and separating their Oreos, I was eating freshly baked bread, cookies straight from the oven and, yes, lots of homemade pies. And I had absolutely no appreciation for it. I wanted Twinkies and Betty Crocker mixes and anything else that came in bright, shiny packaging with lots of preservatives.

Today, I am so grateful to my mother for holding her ground, because it encouraged my sisters and me to start baking. And while it was often pure chaos in our kitchen on a Saturday morning as we practiced our fledgling baking skills, we came to recognize when a cake layer was ready to come out of the oven, what a stiff meringue looked like and how to bake a simple but delicious apple pie. And we learned it all from a baker who learned it from her mother. Who learned it from her mother. Methods and techniques passed down with great love from one generation of bakers to the next.

My baking journey has taken a few detours since my childhood culinary education. I went to college for fashion design but changed course and spent years as an instructional designer and corporate writer in my own business, working mainly for pharmaceutical and food industries. Whether you needed to know the benefits of the latest migraine medication or the proper way to bake a donut, I was your girl. It was a rewarding career, but I was getting restless. The hours were long. The business was changing. So, I did what anyone in my position would do—I started baking pies.

I know. It made no sense, but what started as a mild Pinterest obsession with latticed pies turned into an Instagram account where I found a creative outlet for designs and ideas I didn't even know I had. That turned into an opportunity to collaborate with the Food Network, which led to opportunities to teach pie making and decorating. Still, I felt like I should be looking for a "real job." Then my father died unexpectedly. In shock, I retreated to the kitchen and just baked pie after pie. I know now that it was my way of processing his death and everything he had meant to me. And, after a while, things came back into focus. I was going to follow this pie journey to see where it led. This book is the next step on that path.

My goal with this book is to share what I know about pie decorating and to inspire you to bake a beautiful pie of your own, regardless of your skill level. Each chapter of the book focuses on a different element of pie making and decorating, from working with pie dough (Chapter 1) to exploring specific decorating styles like garden and forest themes; modern looks; braid, twist and weave patterns; and pies for special occasions (Chapters 2 to 6). Once you're feeling confident, I hope you'll up your pie game even further by making one of the stunning showstopper pies in Chapter 7.

Each recipe in this book includes detailed, step-by-step instructions on how to create all the elements. In many cases, step-by-step photos are included to help you. In Chapter 8, you'll find lots of information about general pie-making techniques including rolling out dough, lining a pie plate and blind baking a pie shell. You'll also learn how to braid, lattice and make a decorative edge.

Of course, a pie can't just look beautiful; it has to taste delicious as well. Many of the savory and sweet pie recipes in this book are ones I've been making for years, and I am so happy to share them with you here. They have been carefully chosen not only for their flavors but for their reliability. I hope they will soon become some of your favorite recipes as well.

As you go through this book, please keep a couple of things in mind. Making and decorating pies takes practice and patience. If you're just starting to make pies, don't be hard on yourself if you don't get everything perfect the first time, or the second or the third. I certainly didn't and I still don't. This is a journey like any other. Get a feel for the flour and butter between your fingers and a rolling pin between your hands. Use the techniques and elements that appeal to you and match your skill level. Mix and match the pie tops with the fillings. Scale back on the decorations, add more or mix them up with decorations from other pies you like. There are no rules here. Your creative energy is the only prerequisite for success. After all, pie making and decorating should be an expression of your personality and your style. I hope this book inspires you to take that journey.

Helen
xo

Equipment: A Few of My Favorite Things

There is a dizzying array of tools out there to help you make and decorate pies. Do you need them all? Absolutely not. Here's a rundown on some of my favorite must-have tools along with some nice-to-have equipment that you can pick up as your confidence and abilities grow. Most are inexpensive and are readily available in stores and online.

Essential Tools

Cookie Cutters: Cookie cutters are an easy (and inexpensive) way to pretty-up any pie top. With so many beautiful cookie-cutter shapes to choose from, from tiny flowers and geometric shapes to realistic leaves and novelty shapes, they're a fun and simple way to create a stunning look for your pie.

Craft Paintbrushes/Pastry Brushes: Craft paintbrushes make excellent (and inexpensive) egg wash tools. I especially love the little, thin ones that can get into all the nooks and crannies of my pie decorations. Just make sure that the brushes you use haven't been used for any non–food-related tasks. If you choose to go with a pastry brush, look for one with soft, natural bristles rather than silicone ones, which won't give you an even wash.

Digital Weight Scale: When I teach people to make pie, one of the first things I encourage them to buy (after a rolling pin) is a digital weight scale. Unlike measuring, when you weigh your ingredients you get the same result every time. It also makes recipes easier to scale up and down accurately. The best part of a digital scale is the "tare" feature, which resets the scale to zero. This allows you to weigh all your ingredients in one bowl, simply by hitting tare between each addition.

Food Processor: A food processor is my go-to for making pie dough. Why? Because it has the power to make anyone a pastry hero. Really, it's almost criminal how easy it is to make pie dough in a food processor. That's not to say you can't make pie dough by hand or with a stand mixer, but you can do it faster and with more consistent results with a food processor. Look for a processor that has at least a 10-cup capacity so it can easily accommodate pie dough for a double-crust pie.

Hobby or Utility Knife: A sharp hobby or utility knife with replacement blades is one of the handiest tools you can have in your pie toolbox. With a fine tip and beveled edge, you'll get sharp, accurate cuts in your dough and better control than a standard paring knife can provide.

Offset Spatula: An offset spatula (or palette knife) is one of my favorite pie decorating tools. I use it to transfer pie dough cutouts and other decorations from my work station to my pie without worrying about warming them with my hands or bending them out of shape. It also does double duty as a tool for smoothing the tops of curd and meringue pies and getting filling into every corner of a tart tin. My favorite offset spatula has a 4½-inch (11-cm) blade.

Pie Plate: Pie plates come in all sizes, materials and shapes. At the end of the day, the best pie plate for you is the one you reach for most often (just promise me you'll stay away from those flimsy, disposable tin plates). I love affordable, dark metal plates because they conduct heat rapidly and consistently and give me a crisp, evenly browned crust. Glass pie plates are another good choice as they also conduct heat evenly with the added bonus of allowing you to see your bottom crust browning.

Pie-Crust Shields: These nifty pie-crust savers come in all sorts of materials, from aluminum to silicone, but my personal favorite is a bisphenol A (BPA)-free, U.S. Food and Drug Administration (FDA)-approved silicone pie-crust shield. Unlike rigid aluminum shields, a silicone shield can be adjusted to fit any round 8-inch (20-cm) to 11-inch (28-cm) pie, they are easier to store than metal shields and are light enough to be added and removed without accidentally knocking off pieces of your crust.

Pie Weights: One of my pet peeves is an unnecessary pie tool. Stone or metal pie weights are definitely on that list. I'm not suggesting that you forgo pie weights altogether (it would be challenging to bake a beautifully blind-baked shell without them). Instead, try using uncooked rice or small dried beans. They are inexpensive, reusable, just the right weight and they fit very nicely into the corners and curves of a pie shell.

Rimless Baking Sheets: A rimless baking sheet is my go-to when making pies. If I'm building a pie top on parchment paper, and want to move it to the refrigerator, I can slide the design, parchment paper and all, onto a rimless sheet without disturbing the design. It's also large enough to hold a variety of cutouts and decorations so there are fewer pans to juggle in and out of the refrigerator.

Rolling Pin: There are three basic types of rolling pins. The one you choose is a personal preference. The classic variety, called a baker's or American rolling pin, features a cylindrical wood barrel that rotates around a rod, fitted with ball bearings and a handle at each end. This is my personal favorite because it is comfortable to use and the ball bearings allow for smoother, longer rolls. French-style rolling pins are narrower with tapered ends instead of handles. Because they are one piece, some people like the even control they provide when rolling pie dough. A Shaker-style rolling pin features an untapered wood cylinder with no handles. This type of pin tends to be a bit heavier and can be awkward to use if you're not familiar with it. Regardless of the type, a solid maple wood pin always gets my vote. While marble and ceramic rolling pins look nice, they are much too heavy to use for rolling pie dough.

Ruler: An 18-inch (46-cm), clear plastic ruler is invaluable for everything from determining the width of lattice to setting a straight edge.

Silicone Rolling Mat: These useful rolling mats are nonslip and feature handy imprints of circles in several different diameters as well as ruler markings up the sides to ensure your pie dough is always the right size.

Tart Tins with Removable Bottoms: I love tart tins, especially ones with removable bottoms. They are perfect for curd and fruit tarts, but I like to use them for pies as well. Yes, perhaps it's a bit unconventional, but you can bake a pie exactly the same way in a tart tin as you can in a pie pan and you get the added bonus of having a variety of shapes to choose from. I also never get tired of gazing upon the pretty fluted pie dough edges these tins produce.

Nice-to-Have Tools

Baking Steels/Pizza Stones/Baking Sheet: A baking steel provides a consistent, even heat that helps crisp up the base of the pie before it has a chance to absorb any juices and cause a soggy bottom. Pizza stones also work well, but they don't store as much heat as a baking steel, and cleaning up spills can be messy. A third option is a preheated baking sheet. While it will not get as hot as a steel or stone, it will definitely help prevent filling from seeping through to the bottom of your pie.

Decorating Tweezers: This handy tool makes it easier to move and place small and delicate pie decorations like nonpareils and edible flowers.

Instant-Read Thermometer: Whether you need to check the temperature of caramel or determine whether a pie filling is cooked, an instant-read thermometer makes the job quick and easy.

Impression or Embossing Mats: Traditionally used by cake decorators for fondant-based cakes, impression mats are great for giving your pie tops a "one-of-a-kind" look. Some of my favorite designs include lace patterns, delicate flower designs and woodgrains. Available in a variety of sizes, the best mats are made from silicone, which tend to have the deepest impressions so they hold the final design.

Impression Rolling Pins: These pins are a bit more of an investment than a mat (and take up more room in your kitchen) but they do cover a larger pie dough surface area with a single roll. Depending on the brand and the quality you choose, you may also get deeper impressions than you would with a mat, so your design may hold up better under the heat of the oven. With so many beautiful designs to choose from, they can be hard to resist.

Microplane Zester: I will always choose a microplane zester over a knife or a grater for zesting fruit. I simply can't resist those lovely fluffy piles of fine zest that add just the right amount of texture to curds.

Multi-Wheel Stainless-Steel Lattice Cutters: If you love latticing like I do, this tool is going to make your heart sing. Available in five to seven wheel versions, these cutters are real time savers, letting you cut multiple and consistent-sized strips of pie dough every time. And because the lattice wheels are adjustable in size, you can cut your strips as narrow or as wide as the cutter will allow. Again, you get what you pay for here so look for a cutter that has solid reviews.

Pastry Wheel: A pastry wheel is a sharp cutting wheel with a plain or crimped edge attached to a handle. A sturdy pastry wheel is a great way to save time cutting lattice as it rolls smoothly and quickly across the dough. A crimped wheel will give your lattice a wavy, decorative look. For the best of both worlds, look for a double-headed pastry wheel that features both a straight and crimped wheel.

Stainless-Steel Pizza Peel: I like to build more complicated pie-top designs and lattice designs off the pie. A stainless-steel pizza peel makes it easy to slide the chilled designs safely onto the filled pie shell.

Turntable: While a turntable is not a "have-to-have" pie-making tool, it does make tasks like crimping pies easier. A turntable can be any flat surface that spins, from a lazy Susan to a cake turntable, but the ones that work best are elevated on a stand so you can work at a comfortable level. Turntables are also really useful for creating swirl effects like the one for the Swirlin' Blueberry Mousse Tart on pages 47 to 49.

Setting Up for Success

Learning how to make and decorate pies is a wonderful way to express your creativity through pastry. Here are my top tips for getting you rolling in the right direction.

Chill

After you have rolled out your pie dough, but before you begin cutting your decorative shapes and strips, remember to slide the rolled-out dough onto a baking sheet and into the refrigerator for 5 minutes to chill. A cold piece of dough will reward you with straight strips of lattice, less sticking and cleaner edges to your cutouts. After your decorations are cut, keep them in the refrigerator until you need them. Because they've been kept chilled, they'll be much less likely to rip, flop and tear.

Prop Up Your Decorations

Some of the most impactful pie designs are those that have a 3-D feel to them. But how can you achieve that look when the heat of the oven is likely to soften and flatten your decorations? Here's one way: Use small balls of dough as props under the decoration that you want to keep elevated or curved. The Apple-Cranberry Winter Wreath Pie on pages 155 to 160 uses hidden dough balls to keep the ribbon looking curved and three-dimensional.

Anchor Your Decorations

While it's perfectly okay to move your decorations around while working on your design, once you're happy with the placement, make sure to use a bit of egg wash as "glue" to anchor them to your pie top. That way, when your pie goes in the oven, you can be confident your decorations will stay where they belong.

Lattice off the Pie

In my opinion, there are few things messier than trying to lattice a pie *on* the pie. Inevitably, the filling gets all over the strips. The strips soften. Trying to adjust a strip or two can be an exercise in frustration as the lattice inevitably tears or sinks into the filling. It all makes me very unhappy, which is why I now lattice all my pies far, far away from the filling and shell. Not only is this method less messy (and less stressful), it makes it quicker and easier to readjust the lattice if I need

to. If the strips warm up too much as I'm working, I simply move them to the refrigerator to chill for a few minutes. A step-by-step guide on how to create an off-the-pie lattice is on pages 177 and 178.

Egg Wash in Layers

Egg wash adds shine and enhances the golden color of any baked pie. When working with decorative pies, especially those with multiple layers, getting an even color to the whole pie can be challenging. That's because the heat from the oven tends to brown the top layers first, leaving the decorations beneath pale and sad. To avoid this, I like to egg wash my pie in layers, starting with the base. I then egg wash my decorations as I add them to the pie, giving my baked pie a beautiful and even golden brown color.

Get Creative with Your Pie Vents

Vents let steam escape through the top of the pie crust and help to prevent fruit overflows that can affect the look of your finished pie. Finding spots to create vents in a highly decorative pie takes some ingenuity. Look for spots between (and even under) decorations and braids where you can make a knife cut. Alternatively, bake additional decorations separately that you can then use to cover the vent after the pie is baked. If you notice that your pie is puffing up as it bakes, making some additional vents is usually enough to bring your pie back into line.

Freeze Unbaked Fruit-Filled Pies

Whenever possible, I freeze my fruit-based pies before I bake them. I've found that decorations are less likely to distort and crimps stay crisper that way. Please don't ask me for the science behind it. I only know that it works. While this trick won't work for custard pies (they don't freeze well), freezing does a great job minimizing shrinkage on pie shells that will be blind baked. Before you freeze any pie or shell, be sure to egg wash it and wrap it tightly in plastic wrap. You can then bake your pie, at your convenience, directly from the freezer. For a complete pie, you'll need to add an additional 10 minutes or so to the baking time. A pie shell will blind bake fairly close to the time outlined in the recipe.

Skip the Egg Wash for Colored Pie Dough

I love using freeze-dried ingredients like blueberries and spinach to give my pies a custom look without having to use artificial colors (see the Colorful Pie Doughs recipe on page 27). The downside is that natural colors tend to fade in the heat of the oven. Adding egg wash to these doughs just adds to the problem as it browns the dough as well. For this reason, I recommend giving egg wash a pass for any colored dough elements on your pie.

Keep Your Eye on Your Pie in the Oven

Get in the habit of checking on your pie once it's in the oven to make sure that your decorations are staying where you placed them and that the pie is sufficiently vented. I set my timer to go off every 15 minutes during the baking phase so I can check on my pie's progress and make any necessary adjustments. Yes, it does mean staying near the oven but, after all the hard work you've put into the pie, I think you'll agree it's time well spent.

Pie Fails and Fixes

Here are some of the most common reasons a pie fails to live up to the hype and how to prevent or fix the problem for the next time.

Pie Shell Shrank/Slumped

The most common cause of a shrunken or slumped pie shell is dough that has been overworked and/or didn't have sufficient time to relax. Here are some ways to prevent this problem. Give your pie dough at least 30 minutes in the refrigerator to relax before rolling. Try to avoid rerolling the same piece of pie dough more than twice if possible. Make sure your pie weights reach all the way up the sides of your pie plate and sit firmly up against the side of your shell. Keep in mind that pie dough will always shrink a bit in the oven. The best way I've found to offset this is to bake the shell with a 1-inch (3-cm) dough overhang that is trimmed off with a sharp knife after blind baking. See the Partial and Full Blind Baking section on pages 172 and 173 for the technique.

Fruit Filling Is Runny

If you've followed the recipe and your filling is still runny, chances are you've sliced the pie too soon after baking it. Pie fillings thicken as they cool, so leave the pie for at least 3 hours before digging in. If you'd like to serve the pie warm, gently reheat it in the oven just before serving.

Decorative Border Fell Off in the Oven

If your braid border or decorative edge falls off the pie in the oven, it was likely set too close to the edge of the pie. Recognizing that all pie dough is going to shrink a bit in the oven, always create your border at least ¼ inch (6 mm) from the outer edge of the pie.

Fruit Pie Top Sunk During Baking

Fruit pies sink because the fruit settles and reduces in volume as it bakes. There are a couple of ways to prevent this. Pack the fruit as close together in the shell as you can, with as few gaps as possible. I also find piling the fruit up about ½ inch (13 mm) higher in the center of the pie helps to offset any shrinkage during baking.

Decorations Distorted

Decorations are less likely to distort and crimps are more likely to stay crisper when the pie is frozen before baking. See Setting Up for Success on page 14 for more information on baking frozen pies.

Small Decorations Burned

To prevent burning, avoid egg washing small decorations. Once your pie is in the oven, check on it regularly. If you notice that certain elements are baking too quickly, cover them with pieces of tinfoil.

Baked Tart Is Stuck in the Tart Tin

To prevent the tart from sticking to the tin, try to separate any sugary filling from the tin as soon as the tart comes out of the oven, before the filling has a chance to harden. Because your tart tin likely has a fluted edge, do the best you can by getting the sharp tip of the knife between the pie and the flutes and gently push back any filling overflow. If your tart tin has a removable bottom, wait for the pie to cool and then place the tart tin on top of a wide-mouth drinking glass. Apply gentle pressure evenly on all sides of the tart to encourage the tin to drop away from the base.

Pie Slice Doesn't Come Out Cleanly

If your first slice of pie is always a bit messy, cut a thin sliver first. This will give you enough space to get a lifter under the next slice and lift it cleanly away.

Everyday All-Butter Pie Dough (page 21)

chapter 1

The Pie Doughs

A friend once said to me, "Whoever came up with the saying, 'easy as pie,' has never made pie dough." If that's how you feel, this chapter is for you. If you've never made pie dough, this chapter is for you. If you have no problem making pie dough, well, this chapter is still for you because there are some seriously ah-mazing pie dough recipes within these pages.

Making the perfect pie dough has taken on almost mystical qualities over the years. There have been thousands of articles dedicated to it and hundreds of tears shed when the pie dough hasn't turned out as expected. In the process, it's managed to scare a lot of you off ever trying to make it. But it shouldn't be that way. Making pie dough doesn't have to be hard. It just has to be understood.

This chapter is dedicated to helping you understand what goes into a great pie dough and how you can make it in your kitchen. Today. For your ah-hah moment (sorry, Oprah), read through the A Pie Dough Primer (page 19) and then keep the magic word you find there (you'll know it when you see it) in your head. Read through My Two Methods for Making the Perfect Pie Dough on page 20 and choose the one that feels right for you, your comfort level and the type of pie you are making. Then, pick a pie dough recipe. There are lots of options in this chapter, from all-butter pie dough and butter/shortening combinations to flavored and colored doughs. Each recipe in this book suggests a dough but feel free to substitute with the one that calls your name.

Chocolate Pie Dough (page 21)

A Pie Dough Primer

For me, making pie dough is one of the most rewarding parts of pie making. There's something about watching four simple main ingredients—flour, fat, salt and water—come together to create a buttery, crisp and delicious pie crust that awes me every time. It's also why I feel sad when people say that they find the idea of making pie dough scary.

Contrary to what you may have heard, you don't need a genetic gift, a pastry chef education or decades of experience to make great pie dough. You just need to keep one magic word in your head. Gluten. I know. It's not sexy, but gluten is at the heart of every flaky or tough-as-leather piece of pie crust you will ever eat.

Simply put, gluten is a strong, stretchy protein that is formed when water meets the proteins in wheat or by-products of wheat. Gluten plays an important role in all sorts of baking. We knead bread dough because we want to develop strong gluten strands that will give us that "chew" and elasticity that signals a good-quality bread. In pasta, gluten provides the firm "al dente" or bite. And it gets all the credit for the springy consistency of pizza dough. While we want our pie crust to have the structure that gluten delivers, too much of it will lead to a leathery, chewy pie crust. For that reason alone, most of your pie-dough–making efforts should be focused on one thing: inhibiting gluten development.

Choose the Right Flour

You may have some bread flour lurking at the back of your pantry. That doesn't mean it's a good idea to use it in your favorite pie crust recipe. Not all flours are created equal. Different types of flour have different gluten protein counts. Bread flour has one of the highest percentages of gluten at 12 to 15 percent, making it perfect for bread but not at all suitable for a pie crust. With only 7 to 8 percent gluten, cake flour is a great choice for delivering a moist crumb and fluffy texture to cakes and muffins, but it's too weak for pie dough. Pastry flour has an 8 to 9 percent protein count and can deliver a tender pie crust, albeit one that can be a bit fragile and doesn't hold up to a lot of handling. All-purpose flour is the compromise as it averages 9 to 12 percent gluten, which is still low enough in gluten content to produce a flaky, tender pie crust. The recipes in this book use all-purpose flour for that reason—and because I like the elasticity and strength it offers for latticing and decorations—but feel free to experiment with pastry flour to see which you prefer.

Weigh Your Pie Dough Ingredients

I would marry my digital scale if I could. That is how much I love and trust it. A digital scale will ensure that you have the right measurement of water, the correct amount of flour and the perfect weight of butter cubes to make the pie dough as it was envisioned, written and tested by the creator of the recipe. Getting the measurements right will also avoid excessive gluten production and disappointing dough results. If I haven't convinced you to switch to weight measurements, I strongly encourage you to follow the dip and sweep method for measuring dry ingredients. Simply dip the cup into a container of flour and then sweep the excess off with the back of a knife for an accurate measurement every time.

Think Cold, Cold, Cold

Cold has the power to slow the formation of gluten, which is why keeping your water ice cold is a must if you want flaky, tender pie dough. Chilling your butter stops it from softening and melting. This, in turn, stops the water in the butter from interacting with the flour, which prevents—you got it—gluten. Some pie makers take this cold rule to the extreme by keeping the mixing bowl, the flour, and anything else that comes in contact with pie dough in the refrigerator or freezer. Unless your kitchen is extremely warm, I've never found this to be necessary.

Don't Push Your Pie Dough Around

Your pie dough does not like being overkneaded or overprocessed. It will show its disdain by producing long and strong gluten strands that will make your pie dough tough and leathery. I encourage you to follow the techniques outlined in this book carefully when it comes to making, rolling, transferring and baking pie dough.

Give Your Pie Dough a Rest

You may be tempted to start rolling your dough right after you form it into a disc. Don't do it! Your pie dough needs at least 30 minutes to rest in the refrigerator. This important step allows any gluten that has formed during production to settle down and relax. The reward for your patience will be pie dough that is easier to roll out, doesn't shrink during baking and has a better shot at turning out flaky, tender and delicious.

For my methods of rolling out pie dough, fitting dough to your pie plate or tart tin, and more, see Chapter 8: Essential Pie Skills and Decorating Techniques, starting on page 167.

My Two Methods for Making the Perfect Pie Dough

There are two ways that I make pie dough for decorative pies: with a food processor and using a stand mixer. While dough can be made by hand, I don't recommend it for highly decorative pies like the ones in this book. There is a lot of room for error, which the food processor or stand mixer nearly eliminates. Also, having big chunks of butter in your dough doesn't make for a very pliable and smooth dough when it comes to latticing and cutting decorations. Preparing your dough with a food processor or stand mixer will result in dough that works beautifully for decorations and will give you a consistently tender, flaky pie crust.

By Food Processor

My favorite way to make dough is with a food processor. It's fast (less than 2 minutes), it provides consistent results and it keeps the ingredients cold and out of contact with warm hands. Make sure to use a processor large enough to hold all of the ingredients called for in the recipe. For a double-crust pie, you will need a food processor with at least a 10-cup (2.4-L) capacity.

By Stand Mixer

Like using a food processor, this hands-off method of making pie dough lets the stand mixer do the work while providing you with an evenly hydrated dough that is easy to work with.

Tip

Do not add any more water than what is listed in the pie dough recipe, even if it looks like the mixture is not coming together after you have added all of the liquid. You just need to keep pulsing or mixing. Have faith. It will happen.

To Make Ahead or Store

All the doughs in this chapter can be refrigerated, tightly wrapped, for up to 3 days. Dough can also be frozen, double wrapped in plastic wrap, for up to 3 months. Thaw the disc(s) overnight in the refrigerator before using.

Everyday All-Butter Pie Dough

I call this my workhorse pie dough because it never lets me down. It delivers a tender and flavorful pastry and produces a supple, easy-to-roll dough that doesn't tear or break under the stress of all sorts of pie decorations including latticing. The addition of sugar to this recipe helps to tenderize the dough and adds a golden color to the baked crust.

Fill a small bowl with cold water and ice cubes and set it aside.

Place the flour, sugar and salt into the bowl of a food processor fitted with a metal blade or a stand mixer fitted with a paddle attachment. Pulse two to three times in a food processor or mix on low speed (speed 2) in a stand mixer to combine and distribute the ingredients. Cube the butter into 1-inch (3-cm) pieces. Add these to the bowl. Pulse four to six times in the food processor or mix on low speed (speed 2) in the stand mixer to coat the butter with flour and to cut it into the dry ingredients.

Add the ice water, 1 tablespoon (15 ml) at a time, pulsing two times or mixing on low speed (speed 2) for 15 seconds between each addition. After all of the water has been added, continue to pulse or mix at low speed until the dough just begins to clump together (an additional fifteen to twenty pulses in a food processor or 3 to 4 minutes in a stand mixer).

Turn the dough out onto a lightly floured surface. Cup your hands around the dough and gently bring it together into a ball. If making a double pie crust, cut the ball in half. Press gently with the heel of your hand to flatten the pieces into discs that are 1 inch (3 cm) thick. Wrap each disc tightly in plastic wrap and refrigerate for at least 30 minutes before using.

See photo on page 23.

Variation: Savory Pie Dough

For a single crust, omit the sugar and add ½ teaspoon of freshly ground black or mixed peppercorns to the Everyday All-Butter Pie Dough recipe. For a double crust, omit the sugar and add 1 teaspoon of freshly ground black or mixed peppercorns to the Everyday All-Butter Pie Dough recipe.

Variation: Chocolate Pie Dough (Single Crust)

Reduce the amount of flour to 1 cup (4 ½ oz/128 g) and add 2 tablespoons (½ oz/14 g) of unsweetened cocoa powder. Increase the granulated sugar to 2 tablespoons (1 oz/30 g) and omit the salt.

Single-Crust Pie Dough
Makes one disc, enough for one single-crust, standard 9-inch (23-cm) pie or tart

1¼ cups (5½ oz/155 g) all-purpose flour

2 tsp (⅓ oz/9 g) granulated sugar

½ tsp kosher salt

½ cup (4 oz/113 g) unsalted butter, chilled

3 tbsp (1½ oz/43 g) ice water

Double-Crust Pie Dough
Makes two discs, enough for one double-crust, standard 9-inch (23-cm) pie

2¼ cups (10 oz/284 g) all-purpose flour

1 tbsp (½ oz/14 g) granulated sugar

1 tsp kosher salt

1 cup (8 oz/227 g) unsalted butter, chilled

5 tbsp (2½ oz/71 g) ice water

Flaky Butter-Shortening Pie Dough

I love a flaky pie dough as much as the next person, but I've never been able to get excited about an all-shortening pie dough for one simple reason: It may be flaky, but it lacks flavor. The combination of shortening and butter here delivers the best of both worlds—big time flakiness and flavor. As an added bonus, because shortening has a higher melting point, you can feel confident that decorations and borders made with this pie dough will stay sharp in the oven.

Fill a small bowl with cold water and ice cubes and set it aside.

Place the flour, sugar and salt into the bowl of a food processor fitted with a metal blade or a stand mixer fitted with a paddle attachment. Pulse the mixture two to three times in a food processor or mix on low speed (speed 2) in a stand mixer to combine and distribute the ingredients.

Cube the shortening and butter into 1-inch (3-cm) pieces and add these to the bowl. Pulse the mixture four to six times in the food processor or mix it on low speed (speed 2) in the stand mixer to coat the shortening and butter with the flour and to cut it into the dry ingredients.

Add the ice water, 1 tablespoon (15 ml) at a time, pulsing two times or mixing on low speed (speed 2) for 15 seconds between each addition. After all the water has been added, continue to pulse or mix on low speed until the dough just begins to clump together (an additional fifteen to twenty pulses in a food processor or 3 to 4 minutes in a stand mixer).

Turn the dough out onto a lightly floured surface. Cup your hands around the dough and gently bring it together into a ball. If making a double pie crust, cut the ball in half. Press gently with the heel of your hand to flatten the pieces into discs 1 inch (3 cm) thick. Wrap each disc tightly in plastic wrap and refrigerate for at least 30 minutes before using.

Single-Crust Pie Dough
Makes one disc, enough for a single-crust, standard 9-inch (23-cm) pie or tart

1¼ cups (5½ oz/155 g) all-purpose flour

1½ tsp (¼ oz/6 g) granulated sugar

½ tsp kosher salt

3 tbsp (1½ oz/43 g) vegetable shortening, chilled

⅓ cup (3 oz/85 g) unsalted butter, chilled

3 tbsp (1½ oz/43 g) ice water

Double-Crust Pie Dough
Makes two discs, enough for one double-crust, standard 9-inch (23-cm) pie

2¼ cups (10 oz/284 g) all-purpose flour

1 tbsp (½ oz/14 g) granulated sugar

1 tsp kosher salt

6 tbsp (3 oz/85 g) vegetable shortening, chilled

¾ cup (6 oz/170 g) unsalted butter, chilled

5 tbsp (2½ oz/71 g) ice water

Sweet Tart Dough

Also known as pâté sucrée, this dough is sweeter and crumblier than traditional pie dough. Its cookie-like texture makes it the perfect foundation for fruit, custard and curd tarts.

Place the flour, sugar and salt into a food processor bowl, fitted with a metal blade, or a stand mixer fitted with a paddle attachment. Pulse two to three times in a food processor or mix on low speed (speed 2) in a stand mixer to combine and distribute the ingredients. Cube the butter into 1-inch (3-cm) pieces. Add the butter cubes to the food processor or mixer bowl. Pulse four to six times or mix on low speed (speed 2) to coat the butter with flour and to cut it into the dry ingredients. Add the egg(s) and ice water and continue to pulse or mix on low speed (speed 2) until the dough starts to clump together (about fifteen to twenty pulses in a food processor or 2 to 3 minutes in a mixer).

Turn the dough out onto a lightly floured surface. Cup your hands around the dough and gently bring it together into a ball. If making a double pie crust, cut the ball in half. Press gently with the heel of your hand to flatten the pieces into discs 1 inch (3 cm) thick. Wrap the dough tightly in plastic wrap and refrigerate for at least 30 minutes.

Single-Crust Tart Dough
Makes one disc, enough for one 9-inch (23-cm) tart shell

1¼ cups (5½ oz/155 g) all-purpose flour

3 tbsp (1½ oz/43 g) granulated sugar

¼ tsp kosher salt

½ cup (4 oz/113 g) unsalted butter, chilled

1 large egg, cold, lightly beaten

1½ tbsp (¾ oz/21 g) ice water

Double-Crust Tart Dough
Makes two discs, enough for a double-crust, standard 9-inch (23-cm) tart shell

2½ cups (11 oz/312 g) all-purpose flour

6 tbsp (3 oz/85 g) granulated sugar

½ tsp kosher salt

1 cup (8 oz/227 g) unsalted butter, chilled

2 large eggs, cold, lightly beaten

3 tbsp (1½ oz/43 g) ice water

Citrus-Scented Tart Dough

The addition of orange and lemon zest to this tart dough provides a lovely citrus note that complements spice-forward fillings like the Holiday Lights Mincemeat Tart (page 131).

Fill a small bowl with ice and water and set aside.

Place the flour, icing/confectioners' sugar, orange zest, lemon zest and salt into a food processor bowl fitted with a metal blade or a stand mixer fitted with a paddle attachment. Pulse two to three times in a food processor or mix on low speed (speed 2) in a stand mixer to distribute the ingredients.

Cut the chilled butter into 1-inch (3-cm) pieces. Add the butter cubes to the food processor or mixer bowl. Pulse four to six times or mix on low speed (speed 2) to coat the butter with flour and to cut it into the dry ingredients. Add the ice water, 1 tablespoon (15 ml) at a time, pulsing two times or mixing on low speed (speed 2) for 15 seconds between each addition. After all the water has been added, continue to pulse until the dough starts to clump together (about fifteen to twenty pulses in a food processor or 2 to 3 minutes in a mixer).

Turn the dough out onto a lightly floured surface. Cup your hands around the dough and gently bring it together into a ball. Use the heel of your hand to flatten the ball into a 1-inch (3-cm)-thick disc. Wrap the disc tightly in plastic wrap and refrigerate for at least 30 minutes.

1 cup (4½ oz/128 g) all-purpose flour

⅓ cup (1½ oz/43 g) icing/confectioners' sugar

1 tsp orange zest

1 tsp lemon zest

Pinch of kosher salt

½ cup (4 oz/113 g) unsalted butter, cold

3 tbsp (1½ oz/43 g) ice water

Colorful Pie Doughs

Colored pie doughs are a great way to give your pies a little extra decorating "pop." I use natural colors that will fade a bit in the baking process, but I promise that they will still look beautiful postbake. These beautiful shades of purple, green and gold will also add a hint of flavor to your doughs but, again, most of it will be baked out in the oven.

Master Recipe
Mix the ice water with the color of your choice and transfer it to the refrigerator.

Place the flour, sugar and salt into a food processor bowl fitted with a metal blade or a stand mixer fitted with a paddle attachment. Pulse two to three times in a food processor or mix on low speed (speed 2) in a mixer to combine and distribute the ingredients.

Cut the chilled butter into 1-inch (3-cm) pieces. Add the butter cubes to the food processor or mixer bowl. Pulse four to six times or mix on low speed (speed 2) to coat the butter with flour and cut it into the dry ingredients. Remove the ice water/color mixture from the refrigerator. Add 1 tablespoon (15 ml) of the colored ice water to the mixture and pulse two times/mix on low speed. Continue adding the colored ice water, 1 tablespoon (15 ml) at a time, pulsing two times in a food processor or mixing on low speed in a mixer for 15 seconds between each addition. After all the colored ice water has been added, continue to pulse/mix until the dough just begins to clump and forms into a ball.

Turn the dough out onto a lightly floured surface. Cup your hands around the dough and gently bring it together into a ball. If making a double-crust pie dough, use a knife to cut the ball in half. Press gently with the heel of your hand to flatten each piece into a 1-inch (3-cm)-thick disc. Wrap each disc tightly in plastic wrap and refrigerate for at least 30 minutes.

Deep Purple Blueberry Pie Dough
Whisk together the freeze-dried blueberry powder with the ice water. Mix until thoroughly combined before proceeding with the recipe.

Forest Green Spinach Pie Dough
Whisk together the freeze-dried spinach powder with the ice water. Mix until thoroughly combined before proceeding with the recipe.

Golden Yellow Turmeric Pie Dough
Whisk the turmeric powder with the ice water. Mix until thoroughly combined before proceeding with the recipe.

Single-Crust Pie Dough
Makes one disc, enough for a single-crust, 9-inch (23-cm) pie

3 tbsp (1½ oz/43 g) ice water

1¼ cups (5½ oz/155 g) all-purpose flour

2 tsp (⅓ oz/9 g) granulated sugar

½ tsp kosher salt

½ cup (4 oz/113 g) unsalted butter, chilled

Color of your choice
2 tbsp (¾ oz/22 g) freeze-dried blueberry powder

1 tbsp + 1 tsp (⅕ oz/5 g) freeze-dried spinach powder

1 tsp turmeric

Double-Crust Pie Dough
Makes two discs, enough for a double-crust, 9-inch (23-cm) pie

5 tbsp (2½ oz/71 g) ice water

2¼ cups (10 oz/284 g) all-purpose flour

1 tbsp + 1 tsp (¾ oz/21 g) granulated sugar

1 tsp kosher salt

1 cup (8 oz/227 g) unsalted butter, chilled

Color of your choice
4 tbsp (1½ oz/44 g) freeze-dried blueberry powder

3 tbsp (⅓ oz/9 g) freeze-dried spinach powder

2 tsp (⅕ oz/6 g) turmeric

Vintage Flowers Chocolate Cherry Bakewell Tart (page 37)

chapter 2

Garden Designs

From the bright and cheery face of a sunflower to the swaying, feathery fronds of a fern, the garden provides endless inspiration and possibilities. The floral and botanical designs I've chosen for this chapter will give you lots of opportunity to practice latticing, use cutters and impression mats, work with colored pie dough and use everyday tools to create beautiful and unique looks.

Climbing Roses Peach Slab Pie

Featured Decorations: Embossed Lattice, Pie Dough Roses, Peach Roses

Make the Pie Shell

Cut a piece of parchment paper at least 14 inches (36 cm) long. Flip the jelly roll pan over and mark the outline of a 9 x 13–inch (23 x 33–cm) rectangle on the parchment paper. Set aside. You will use this later to build your lattice top.

Remove two discs of the Everyday All-Butter Pie Dough from the refrigerator. Cut one of the discs in half and return one half to the refrigerator (you will use it later in the recipe). Leave the other half-disc and the second disc on the counter to soften for about 10 minutes. Place the half-disc under the whole disc, and roll out the dough to a 12 x 16–inch (30 x 41–cm) rectangle, approximately ⅛ inch (3 mm) thick. Softening the dough helps the two pieces come together, but if they aren't quite combining, leave them for a few minutes longer to soften more.

Line the jelly roll pan with the dough, following the technique in the Lining a Pie Plate or Tin section on pages 170 and 171, and trimming the overhang to about ½ inch (13 mm). Transfer the pie shell to the refrigerator.

Make the Lattice

Remove the third disc of Everyday All-Butter Pie Dough from the refrigerator and add any leftover dough scraps from the pie shell to it. On a lightly floured piece of parchment paper, roll the dough out to an 11 x 16–inch (28 x 41–cm) rectangle. Using an impression mat or embossed roller, emboss the dough, being sure to press evenly and firmly on the mat or roller to ensure a consistent design.

Using a sharp knife and ruler or a lattice cutter, cut ten 1 x 16–inch (3 x 41–cm) strips. Trim the strips to the following lengths: two 1 x 16–inch (3 x 41–cm) strips, four 1 x 10–inch (3 x 25–cm) strips and four 1 x 5–inch (3 x 13–cm) strips. Slide the lattice pieces with the parchment paper under them onto a baking sheet and set aside. Reroll the scraps of dough into a 4 x 14–inch (10 x 36–cm) rectangle.

Using a pastry crimping wheel, cut eight ½ x 14–inch (13-mm x 36-cm) dough strips and trim to four 1 x 8–inch (3 x 20–cm) strips and four ½ x 12–inch (13-mm x 30-cm) strips. Add the crimped strips to your baking sheet of lattice strips. Transfer the baking sheet to the refrigerator to chill.

(Continued)

I may be a wildflower girl at heart, but I always have time for roses. Specifically, big, beautiful bouquets of flaky, delicious pie dough and peach roses. Team these beauties with an embossed lattice and gingery peach pie filling and you've got a stunning pie that's almost too pretty to eat. Almost.

Makes one double-crust, 9 x 12-inch (23 x 30-cm) slab pie

4 discs, Everyday All-Butter Pie Dough (page 21), chilled

4½ lb (2 kg) fresh, ripe peaches (10 to 12 medium peaches)

⅔ cup (145 g) packed brown sugar

¼ cup (32 g) cornstarch or tapioca flour

1 tbsp (15 ml) fresh lemon juice

2 tsp (4 g) fresh, minced ginger

1 tsp ground cinnamon

1 large egg

1 tsp milk

Equipment

9 x 13–inch (23 x 33–cm) jelly roll pan, about 1 inch (3 cm) deep

Impression mat or embossed rolling pin

Ruler

Pastry crimping wheel

1½-inch (4-cm) circle cutter

1- or 1½-inch (3- or 4-cm) leaf cutter

Climbing Roses Peach Slab Pie (Continued)

Make the Pie Dough Roses and Leaves

Line a baking sheet with parchment paper and set aside. Remove the fourth disc of Everyday All-Butter Pie Dough from the refrigerator. On a lightly floured surface, roll the disc out to a 12-inch (30-cm) circle, approximately ⅛ inch (3 mm) thick.

Using a 1½-inch (4-cm) circle cookie cutter, cut as many rounds as possible from the rolled-out pie dough. Gather and reroll the scraps and cut out more rounds. You will need approximately 60 rounds. Set aside the leftover scraps of dough.

Lay five cut rounds in a row, each one overlapping the next slightly. Starting at the short end of the row, roll up the rounds into a tube shape (photo A). Place the tube on its side and cut it in half to create two roses (photo B). To make the roses look more natural, use your fingertips to separate the petals (photo C). Set the roses on the baking sheet and repeat with the remaining rounds of dough. You will need about 24 pie dough roses.

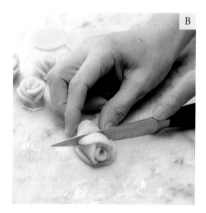

Gather up the leftover pie dough scraps and reroll them to an ⅛-inch (3-mm) thickness. Using a 1- or 1½-inch (3- or 4-cm) leaf cutter, cut ten to twelve leaves. Place the leaves on the baking sheet with the roses and transfer to the refrigerator.

Make the Peach Filling

Fill a large bowl with ice cubes and cold water. Set aside. Fill a 4-quart (3.8-L) saucepan to the halfway point with water and place it on the stovetop. Turn the heat to high and bring the water to a boil.

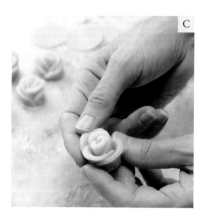

While waiting for the water to boil, use a sharp knife to lightly score an X on the bottom of each peach. When the water is boiling, use a pair of tongs or slotted spoon to carefully slide four or five peaches into the boiling water. Leave them there for 30 to 40 seconds, or until the peach skin at the X mark starts to pull away from the flesh of the peach.

Remove the peaches from the boiling water with tongs or a slotted spoon and immediately plunge them into the prepared ice bath to stop the cooking process. After 15 seconds, remove the peaches from the ice water and place on a clean towel. Starting at the X on each peach, use a paring knife to peel the skin from each peach. The skins should come off easily. If they are being stubborn, use a vegetable peeler or knife to peel away the skin. Repeat the boiling and cooling process for the remaining peaches.

Set aside two peaches for the peach rose decorations you will make later. Halve and pit the remainder of the peaches, then cut them into ¼-inch (6-mm) wedges. Place them in a large bowl. Add the brown sugar, cornstarch or tapioca flour, lemon juice, minced ginger and cinnamon. Stir gently to thoroughly combine and set the bowl aside.

Make the Peach Roses

Remove the remaining half-disc of pie dough from the refrigerator. Roll it out to a 6 x 12–inch (15 x 30–cm) rectangle, approximately ⅛ inch (3 mm) thick. Cut the dough into six 2 x 6–inch (5 x 15–cm) strips. Lay the strips horizontally in front of you. Cut the two reserved peaches in half and discard the stone. On a cutting board, thinly slice each peach in half, crosswise, into ten to twelve slices (thinner slices will bend more easily).

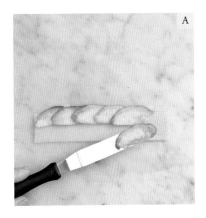

Lay six to eight peach slices in an overlapping row across the top half of each strip of pie dough, ensuring that the dome side of each peach slice is facing up and extends slightly over the dough (photo A). Fold the bottom half of the dough strip up and over the top half to enclose the sliced peaches and press firmly on the strip to seal it (photo B). Starting at one end, gently roll up the peach slices and dough strip to create a single peach rose (photo C). Add the finished peach roses to the baking sheet of pie dough roses in the refrigerator.

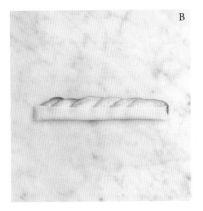

Build the Lattice Top

Place the parchment paper with the outline of the jelly roll pan you made earlier on a flat surface, marked side down but ensuring that you can still see the outline through it.

Remove the tray of lattice strips from the refrigerator. Lay a 16-inch (41-cm) embossed strip of dough diagonally across the pan outline, running from the top right-hand corner to the bottom left-hand corner. Lay four more dough strips on either side of this strip, spacing evenly, alternating embossed and crimped strips, and using progressively shorter strips as you go. Weave in the remaining nine strips, at right angles to the first set (see the Latticing a Pie section on pages 177 and 178 for detailed instructions), using the same alternating pattern of embossed and crimped strips. Slide the parchment paper, with the lattice on it, onto a baking sheet and transfer it to the freezer for 15 minutes.

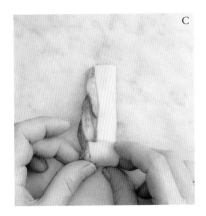

(Continued)

Climbing Roses Peach Slab Pie (Continued)

Assemble the Pie

In a small bowl, whisk together the egg and milk to make the egg wash. Set aside.

Remove the pie shell from the refrigerator and fill it with the peach mixture. Brush the pie edges with egg wash.

Remove the lattice top from the freezer. Slide a pizza lifter or large spatula under the lattice and gently move it onto the prepared pie shell. Center the design on the pie top. The lattice top will be quite stiff, making it easy to adjust. When you are happy with the alignment, and the lattice strips have softened a bit, fold the ends of the strips under the rim of the pie pan and press firmly to secure. Trim the excess dough.

Place the roses decoratively on a diagonal across the lattice, alternating peach and pie dough roses. Tuck the pie dough leaves under the roses, bending and shaping them as you go. Place the decorated pie in the freezer for 30 minutes.

Bake the Pie

Adjust the oven rack to the lower-middle position and place a baking sheet on it. Preheat the oven to 425°F (220°C).

Remove the pie from the freezer and brush the lattice and pie dough roses gently with the egg wash. Place the pie in the oven on the preheated baking sheet and bake for 15 minutes. Reduce the temperature to 375°F (190°C) and bake for another 50 to 55 minutes, or until the pastry is golden brown and the filling is bubbling between the roses. Remove the pie from the oven.

Allow the pie to set by cooling for at least 3 hours before serving.

To Make Ahead or Store

The pie can be baked 1 day ahead and stored at room temperature, loosely covered. Leftover pie can be covered and stored at room temperature for up to 2 days.

The unbaked pie may be frozen, egg washed and double wrapped, for up to 3 months. It must be baked from frozen. You may need to add an additional 10 to 15 minutes to the baking time for frozen pies.

Vintage Flowers Chocolate Cherry Bakewell Tart

Featured Decoration: Almond Flowers

A classic British Bakewell tart features a flaky pastry base, a healthy layer of jam topped with a rich, nutty frangipane (almond cream) filling. For this version, I've amped things up by including some dark chocolate in the filling for added fudginess, and homemade cherry jam for a Black Forest cake–like experience. Feel free to skip the jam-making process entirely by going with your favorite store-bought jam, but don't forget to make the pretty almond flowers on top. They're my favorite part.

Make the Cherry Jam

Combine the cherries, 1¼ cups (250 g) of the sugar and the lemon juice in a medium saucepan over medium-high heat. Stir until the mixture comes to a boil. Lower the heat and simmer for another 20 minutes, or until the jam thickens. Allow the jam to cool completely before using.

Make and Partially Blind Bake the Tart Shell

Adjust the oven rack to the lower-middle position and place a baking sheet on it. Preheat the oven to 400°F (205°C). Remove the disc of Everyday All-Butter Pie Dough from the refrigerator and, on a lightly floured surface, roll it out to a 12-inch (30-cm) circle. Line the tart tin with the dough, following the technique in the Lining a Pie Plate or Tin section on pages 170 to 171, and leaving a 1-inch (3-cm) overhang. Return any dough scraps to the refrigerator. Partially blind bake the shell following the technique in the Partial and Full Blind Baking section on pages 172 and 173. After baking, allow the shell to cool slightly, then trim the excess pie dough overhang with a sharp knife.

Make the Filling

Lower the oven temperature to 375°F (190°C) and return the baking sheet to the oven. Place the chopped chocolate in a small microwavable bowl and microwave on medium for 15 seconds, then stir. Return the chocolate to the microwave and continue microwaving in 15-second increments, stirring after each increment, until the chocolate is completely melted. Alternatively, melt the chocolate in a double boiler on the stovetop. Set the melted chocolate aside.

Beat the butter and ⅓ cup (66 g) of the sugar in the bowl of an electric mixer with a paddle attachment on medium-high speed until light and fluffy, about 3 minutes. Lower the speed to medium and add the eggs, one at a time, beating for 1 minute between each addition. Add the vanilla extract and beat on medium speed for 1 minute to incorporate. Remove the bowl from the mixer and, using a spatula, fold in the ground almonds and all-purpose flour until just combined (do not overmix). Drizzle in the melted chocolate, gently folding until it is fully incorporated.

(Continued)

Makes one single-crust, 9-inch (23-cm) round tart

1 lb (454 g) dark sweet cherries, fresh or frozen, pitted and cut in half

1¼ cups + ⅓ cup (316 g) granulated sugar, divided

2 tsp (10 ml) lemon juice

1 disc Everyday All-Butter Pie Dough (page 21), chilled

½ cup (100 g) semisweet dark chocolate, chopped

½ cup (120 g) unsalted butter, softened

2 large eggs

1 tsp pure vanilla extract

1¼ cups (120 g) ground almonds or almond meal

2 tbsp (15 g) all-purpose flour

½ cup (45 g) sliced almonds

Equipment

9-inch (23-cm) round tart tin with removable bottom, about 1 inch (3 cm) deep

Small flower cutter, optional

Vintage Flowers Chocolate Cherry Bakewell Tart (Continued)

Assemble and Decorate the Tart

Place 8 tablespoons (160 g) of the cherry jam on the bottom of the tart shell and spread it evenly. Spoon the chocolate almond filling on top of the jam and smooth it with an offset spatula, being sure to spread the filling all the way to the edges.

Using your fingers or a small offset spatula, press the sliced almonds lightly into the top of the filling in a circular flower pattern, with the narrow ends of the almonds pointed inward. Using the leftover dough from the refrigerator, roll out a round to a ⅛-inch (3-mm) thickness. Use a small flower cutter to create the center to each flower, and press one gently into the center of each almond flower. Alternatively, roll little balls of dough as the center for each almond flower.

Bake the Tart

Place the decorated tart on the preheated baking sheet in the oven. Bake for 35 to 40 minutes, or until the tart has risen and feels firm to the touch. Allow the tart to cool completely before unmolding it from the tin and serving, about 1 hour.

To Make Ahead or Store

The tart can be baked 1 day ahead and stored at room temperature, loosely covered. Leftover tart can be covered tightly and stored in the refrigerator for up to 3 days.

Sunflower Rum Raisin-Apple Pie

Featured Decorations: Pie Dough Sunflowers & Leaves, Crimping

Prepare the Rum Raisins and Pie Shell

Place the golden raisins in a small bowl. Pour the rum over the raisins and allow them to soak for 1 hour.

Remove one disc of the Everyday All-Butter Pie Dough from the refrigerator. On a lightly floured surface, roll it out to a 12-inch (30-cm) circle. Transfer and fit it to the pie plate, following the technique in the Lining a Pie Plate or Tin section on pages 170 and 171, and leaving a 1-inch (3-cm) overhang. Gather the leftover dough scraps and set aside. Place the pie shell in the refrigerator while you make the sunflowers and prepare the filling.

Make the Sunflower Leaves

Line a baking sheet with parchment paper. Roll out the scraps of dough left over from the pie shell to a round that is ⅛ inch (3 mm) thick. Cut four 2½-inch (6-cm) hearts and one 3½-inch (9-cm) heart. With a hobby or paring knife, make small V-shaped cuts all along the edges of the hearts to make them look like leaves. Using the back of a knife or a veining tool, mark veins on each of the leaves (photo A). Add the leaves to the baking sheet and set aside.

Make the Sunflower Petals

Remove the disc of Golden Yellow Turmeric Pie Dough from the refrigerator and roll it out to a 12-inch (30-cm) circle. Cut thirty-one 1½-inch (4-cm) petals. Use the comb and scallop tool to mark creases on all the petals (photo B). Add the finished petals to the baking sheet with the leaves. Set the baking sheet aside.

(Continued)

 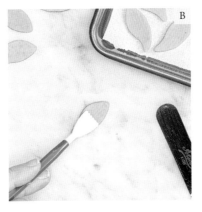

There are few flowers as recognizable as a sunflower. With their cheery yellow petals, big open faces and towering presence, they are hard to ignore. When I received a big, beautiful bouquet of these flowers as a gift, I knew I had to re-create them in pie form. Steeping the raisins in spiced rum adds a complexity to the apple filling, but you can forgo it if you prefer an alcohol-free pie. A little turmeric-tinted pastry gives this beauty its magnificent color without affecting the taste of the baked pie.

Makes one double-crust, 9-inch (23-cm) round pie

½ cup (80 g) golden raisins

3 tbsp (45 ml) dark spiced rum

2 discs Everyday All-Butter Pie Dough (page 21), chilled

1 disc Golden Yellow Turmeric Pie Dough (page 27), chilled

1 disc Chocolate Pie Dough (page 21), chilled, optional (see Note)

¼ cup (32 g) tapioca starch or cornstarch

⅔ cup (145 g) light brown sugar, packed

1 tsp cinnamon

Pinch of kosher salt

3 lb (1.4 kg) apples (Gala, Spy, Cortland, Golden Delicious or a mix), peeled, cored and cut into ¼-inch (6-mm) slices

1 tbsp (15 ml) lemon juice

1 large egg

1 tsp milk

Sunflower Rum Raisin-Apple Pie
(Continued)

Make the Sunflower Center

Remove the disc of Chocolate Pie Dough from the refrigerator. Cut off a quarter of the disc and return the rest to the refrigerator for another use. On a lightly floured surface, roll out the pie dough to a 5-inch (13-cm) circle. Press the dough against the dome side of a sieve to achieve a screened impression. Lay the embossed dough flat on a lightly floured surface and cut one 2½-inch (6-cm) circle (photo C). Using the sharp tines of a fork, make a ¾-inch (2-cm) border around the circumference of the circle, being careful not to poke through the dough. Transfer the sunflower center to the baking sheet.

Assemble the Sunflower

On a piece of parchment paper, mark a 2½-inch (6-cm) circle. Turn the parchment over (ensuring you can see the circle through it). Remove the baking sheet with the sunflower components from the refrigerator. Arrange a row of fourteen petals around the marked circle, positioning the top edge of the petals slightly inside the circle edge. Dab a bit of water along the base of the leaves. Add a second layer of fourteen petals, offsetting them to the petals on the bottom layer and pressing down slightly to adhere them to the first layer (photo D). Dab more water along the base of the second row of leaves. Center the 2½-inch (6-cm) chocolate circle over the petals and press down lightly to seal it to the petals.

Slide the parchment paper with the sunflower on it back onto the baking sheet, along with the three leftover petals, and transfer it to the refrigerator.

Make the Filling

In a medium bowl, whisk together the tapioca flour or cornstarch, brown sugar, cinnamon and salt. Add the apples, raisins and rum and lemon juice and stir to thoroughly combine. Set the bowl aside.

(Continued)

Standard 9-inch (23-cm) round pie plate, about 1¼ inches (3 cm) deep

2½-inch (6-cm) heart cutter

3½-inch (9-cm) heart cutter

1½-inch (4-cm) petal cutter

Comb and scallop fondant tool

Wire sieve

2½-inch (6-cm) circle cutter

Veining tool, optional

Sunflower Rum Raisin-Apple Pie
(Continued)

Assemble the Pie

In a small bowl, whisk together the egg and milk to make the egg wash. Set aside.

Remove the pie shell from the refrigerator and spoon in the rum raisin apple filling.

Remove the second disc of Everyday All-Butter Pie Dough from the refrigerator and roll it out to a 12-inch (30-cm) circle. Brush the edges of the pie shell with some egg wash. Loosely wrap the dough around the rolling pin and gently unroll it onto the filling. Trim the overhang to 1 inch (3 cm). Working around the edge of the pie, fold the overhang from the top crust over and under the bottom pie dough to create a thick border and seal the pie edge. Crimp the border using the technique shown in the Crimping a Pie Edge section on page 179.

Brush the entire pie top with the egg wash. Remove the baking sheet of decorations from the refrigerator. Place the sunflower leaves in a clockwise direction around the pie. Brush the leaves with some egg wash. Using an offset spatula, gently transfer the finished sunflower from the baking sheet to the pie, using the photo as a reference for positioning. Place the three leftover petals loosely on top of the leaves. Do not egg wash the turmeric dough as the color will bleed onto the butter dough.

Use a sharp knife to make slits (vents) under or between the petals and leaves where they will not be seen. Return the pie to the freezer for at least 30 minutes. While the pie is in the freezer, adjust the oven rack to the lower-middle position and place a baking sheet on it. Preheat the oven to 425°F (220°C).

Bake the Pie

Place the pie in the oven on the preheated baking sheet and bake for 15 minutes. Turn the oven down to 375°F (190°C) and continue baking for another 50 to 60 minutes, or until the crust is golden brown. Allow the pie to set by cooling for 3 hours before serving.

To Make Ahead or Store

The pie can be baked 1 day ahead and stored at room temperature, loosely covered. Leftover pie can be covered and stored at room temperature for up to 2 days.

Note:

Because this recipe uses only a small amount of chocolate dough for the sunflower center, it is a perfect use for leftover dough from another project. If you prefer, you may use leftover Everyday All-Butter Pie Dough or Golden Yellow Turmeric Pie Dough from this project to make the sunflower center.

Tropical Pineapple Curd Tart

Featured Decoration: Dried Pineapple Flowers

Make the Pineapple Flowers

Set the oven rack to the lowest part of the oven. Line a baking sheet with parchment paper. Preheat the oven to 200°F (95°C). On a cutting board, place the pineapple on its side and, using a sharp knife, remove the top and the bottom. Stand the pineapple up and carefully remove all of the rind, working top to bottom. Use a potato peeler or knife to remove all the pineapple "eyes." Do not skip this step as this is what will add the "frill" to the edges of your flowers.

Turn the pineapple back on its side and, using a mandolin or a sharp knife, cut ten very thin rounds of pineapple, approximately ⅛ inch (3 mm) thick (photo A). Pat both sides of the rounds dry with a paper towel.

Place the pineapple slices on the parchment-lined baking sheet and transfer the sheet to the oven. Bake for 2½ to 3 hours, until the pineapple flowers are dry and curled at the edges but still pliable.

Remove the pineapple slices from the oven and, while they are still warm, place them inside a muffin tin to help them form the flower shape. Leave the flowers to cool completely at room temperature before removing (photo B). The pineapple flowers can be made up to 24 hours in advance, stored in an airtight container on the countertop.

(Continued)

With its vibrant, sweet fruit curd, a nutty coconut crust and fluffy, marshmallowy meringue, this tart is like a piña colada on a plate.

Makes one single-crust, 4 x 13½-inch (10 x 34.5-cm) rectangular tart

Pineapple Flowers
1 whole, ripe pineapple

Coconut Macaroon Tart Shell
Butter or cooking spray, for greasing

2 cups (185 g) sweetened, finely shredded coconut

2 large egg whites

¼ cup (50 g) granulated sugar

Pineapple Curd
1 tbsp (15 ml) cold water

½ tsp powdered, unflavored gelatin

6 tbsp (84 g) unsalted butter, chilled, cut into ½-inch (13-mm) cubes

½ cup (120 ml) pineapple juice (canned only)

⅓ cup (66 g) granulated sugar

3 large eggs

Pinch of kosher salt

Meringue
1 large egg white

⅓ cup (75 g) superfine sugar (see Note)

¼ cup (37 g) fresh blueberries, optional

Equipment
Regular-size muffin tin

4 x 13½-inch (10 x 34.5–cm) rectangular tart with removable bottom, about 1 inch (3 cm) deep

Kitchen blowtorch, optional

Tropical Pineapple Curd Tart (Continued)

Make the Coconut Macaroon Tart Shell
Adjust the oven rack to the lower-middle position and place a baking sheet on it. Preheat the oven to 350°F (175°C). Grease the tart tin lightly with butter or cooking spray. In a medium bowl, combine the coconut, egg whites and sugar. Press the mixture evenly into the sides and bottom of the tin. Bake the shell on the preheated baking sheet for 15 to 20 minutes, or until golden brown. Allow the crust to cool while you make the pineapple curd.

Make the Pineapple Curd
Place the cold water in a medium bowl. Sprinkle the gelatin evenly over the water. Wait 5 minutes for the gelatin to bloom, then place the butter cubes over the gelatin. Position a fine-mesh sieve over the bowl and set it aside.

In a saucepan, whisk the pineapple juice, sugar, eggs and salt over medium-low heat, stirring constantly, until the sugar is dissolved. Continue to cook, stirring constantly, until the first bubble bursts through the surface, about 6 to 8 minutes. Immediately remove the mixture from the heat and pour it through the sieve. Use a wooden spoon or spatula to press as much of the mixture as possible through the sieve. Remove the sieve and whisk the pineapple-gelatin mixture by hand for 1 minute to ensure that all the gelatin is dissolved, the butter is melted and the mixture is thoroughly combined.

Pour the curd into the cooled coconut macaroon shell. Cover the tart loosely with tinfoil, being careful not to let the tinfoil touch the curd (plastic wrap will stick to the surface and leave marks). Refrigerate for at least 1 hour (or until set) and up to 24 hours.

Make the Meringue
Using a hand mixer, or in the bowl of an electric mixer, beat the egg white on a medium speed until soft peaks form, about 2 minutes. Add the sugar, 1 tablespoon (13 g) at a time, beating thoroughly between additions. After all the sugar has been added, continue beating until the meringue is stiff and shiny and the sugar has completely dissolved, about 7 to 10 minutes. To test whether the sugar has dissolved, rub a bit of meringue between your fingers. If the meringue feels gritty, continue beating until the mixture feels smooth.

Decorate the Tart
Using a tablespoon, place dollops of meringue along the length of the curd tart, spacing them approximately 1 inch (3 cm) apart so that some of the curd is still visible beneath them. Using a kitchen blowtorch, brown the meringue, using a continuous circular motion about 1 to 2 inches (3 to 5 cm) away from the meringue to keep it from burning. Alternatively, place the oven rack in the middle position and preheat the oven to 350°F (175°C). Place the tart in the oven and bake, keeping a close watch on it, until the meringue is nicely browned, about 10 to 12 minutes.

Place the pineapple flowers decoratively on top of and between the meringue dollops. Place the fresh blueberries, if using, around the pineapple flowers. Unmold the tart from the tin and serve cold or at room temperature.

To Make Ahead or Store
The tart is best eaten the day it is made. Cover and store leftovers in the refrigerator for up to 1 day.

Note:
You can make your own superfine sugar by processing granulated sugar in a food processor bowl for 2 to 3 minutes.

Swirlin' Blueberry Mousse Tart

Featured Decoration: Swirls

Make the Gingersnap Tart Shell

Adjust the oven rack to the lower-middle position and preheat the oven to 350°F (175°C). In a medium bowl, mix the gingersnap crumbs and sugar with a fork. Add the melted butter and continue to mix until thoroughly combined.

Press the crumb mixture evenly into the bottom and up the sides of the tart tin. Transfer the shell to the freezer and chill for 10 minutes. Transfer the shell to the oven and bake for 15 minutes, or until the crumb mixture is set. Remove the crust from the oven and allow it to cool completely.

Make the Blueberry Mousse

Place the cold water in a medium bowl. Sprinkle the gelatin evenly over the water. Set a sieve over the bowl. Set aside.

In a medium saucepan, combine the sugar and the blueberries (including juices if using frozen blueberries). Bring to a simmer over low heat, stirring occasionally to break up pieces of the blueberries, until the blueberries have softened and broken down, and the liquid has thickened (about 15 minutes). Remove from the heat and immediately pour the mixture through the sieve over the gelatin. Press on the solids to get as much blueberry mixture through as possible. Remove the sieve and discard the solids.

Whisk the blueberry-gelatin mixture for 1 minute to ensure all the gelatin has dissolved. Set aside to cool, approximately 20 minutes.

While the blueberry mixture is cooling, place the heavy cream and confectioners' sugar in a mixing bowl. Using a stand mixer with a whisk attachment or a hand mixer, beat at medium-high speed until firm peaks form, 2 to 3 minutes. With a rubber spatula, gently fold in one-quarter of the cooled blueberry mixture. Add the remainder of the blueberry mixture and continue to fold gently until fully combined. Pour the blueberry mousse over the gingersnap crust and smooth using an offset spatula. Cover the tart loosely with tinfoil, being sure not to let the tinfoil touch the mousse (plastic wrap will stick to the mousse surface and leave marks) and refrigerate for at least 1 hour and up to 24 hours.

(Continued)

Growing up, my mother would make mousse for special occasions. I remember thinking that its light and airy texture was one of the most decadent things I'd ever tasted. Years later, there's still something about mousse that makes me feel that way. For this tart, I've matched the bright flavor of blueberries in the mousse with the spicy crunch of a gingersnap crust. Pile more fresh blueberries, some pretty nonpareils and edible flowers on top, and finish it with a swirling flourish.

Makes one 9-inch (23-cm) round tart

Gingersnap Tart Shell

1½ cups (170 g) finely ground gingersnap cookie crumbs (from 25 to 30 cookies)

2 tbsp (25 g) granulated sugar

5 tbsp (70 g) unsalted butter, melted

Blueberry Mousse

¼ cup (60 ml) cold water

1 tsp powdered, unflavored gelatin

½ cup (100 g) granulated sugar

12 oz (340 g) fresh or frozen blueberries (thaw completely if using frozen)

1¼ cups (300 ml) heavy cream, cold

2 tbsp (16 g) confectioners' sugar

Swirlin' Blueberry Mousse Tart (Continued)

Decorate the Tart

To create the swirl effect on the top of the dessert, place the cooled tart on a cake turntable. Place the tip of a small offset spatula on the outer edge of the blueberry mousse, on a slight angle. Turn the turntable, using a consistent speed, and let the spatula drag, moving it toward the center of the mousse as you turn.

To create the blueberry half-wreath, place an outline of blueberries on the tart in the general shape of the arc you would like to create. When you are happy with the position, fill in the shape with more blueberries, piling them in layers. Use edible flowers, sprinkles, nonpareils and/or meringue kisses to add texture and color to your wreath. Unmold the tart and serve.

To Make Ahead or Store

The tart is best eaten on the day it is made. Leftovers can be stored, tightly covered in the refrigerator, for up to 2 days.

Blueberry Half-Wreath Decorations

6 oz (170 g) fresh blueberries

Edible flowers, nonpareils, meringue kisses or other decorations, as desired

Equipment

9-inch (23-cm) round tart tin with removable bottom, about 1 inch (3 cm) deep

Cake turntable

Summer Lemon Curd
Fruit Wreath Tart

Featured Decoration: Pie Dough Flowers

Make the Tart Shell

In a small bowl, whisk together the egg and milk to make the egg wash. Set aside.

Adjust the oven rack to the lower-middle position. Preheat the oven to 350°F (175°C). Line a baking sheet with parchment paper. Remove one disc of Sweet Tart Dough from the refrigerator. On a lightly floured surface, roll it out to a 12-inch (30-cm) circle. Transfer and fit the dough to the tart tin, following the technique in the Lining a Pie Plate or Tin section on pages 170 and 171, being sure to build up enough of an edge thickness to hold the flower decorations, about ¼ inch (6 mm), and trimming the edges back to the rim of the tart tin. Set aside.

Remove the second disc of Sweet Tart Dough from the refrigerator and add the dough scraps from the pie shell to it. On a lightly floured surface, roll out the dough to a 12-inch (30-cm) circle. Using the ½-inch (13-mm) flower cutter, cut out 56 small flowers. Using the 1-inch (3-cm) flower cutter, cut out six flowers. Gather up the dough scraps, wrap in plastic wrap and refrigerate or freeze for another use.

Brush the trimmed edges of the pie shell with the egg wash. Place the ½-inch (13-mm) flowers around the rim, keeping them about ⅛ inch (3 mm) inside the metal tart edge (without touching it) to reduce the risk of breakage if the pie shrinks slightly. Place the tart shell in the freezer for at least 15 minutes. In the meantime, place the 1-inch (3-cm) flowers on the parchment-lined baking sheet and bake for 10 to 12 minutes, or until golden brown. Set aside to cool.

Remove the pie shell from the freezer and fully blind bake it following the instructions in the Partial and Full Blind Baking section on pages 172 and 173. Allow it to cool completely.

(Continued)

Every year, I look forward to the bonanza of local fruits that hits the markets in late June. This stunning table topper showcases the best of local summer fruit on an easy-to-make curd tart. The deep yellow curd in this tart is smooth and zingy, with whole eggs giving it a thicker, more luxurious end result. Feel free to use your favorite berries or substitute other curd flavors (raspberry would be heavenly) to make this wreath your very own.

Makes one single-crust, 9-inch (23-cm) round tart

Tart Shell

1 large egg

1 tsp milk

2 discs Sweet Tart Dough (page 24)

Lemon Curd

½ cup (120 ml) fresh lemon juice

2 tsp (4 g) lemon zest, finely grated

¾ cup (150 g) granulated sugar

⅛ tsp kosher salt

3 large eggs

½ cup (120 g) unsalted butter, cubed

Decorations

½ pint (148 g) blueberries

1 pint (weight varies) each of blackberries, strawberries, and goldenberries (see Note), whole

1 cup (155 g) sweet cherries, cut in half, pitted

Edible flowers, optional

Summer Lemon Curd Fruit Wreath Tart (Continued)

Make the Lemon Curd

Place a sieve over a medium bowl and set aside. To a nonreactive medium saucepan, add the lemon juice, lemon zest, granulated sugar, salt and eggs and whisk until well blended. Heat the mixture on medium-low, whisking constantly, until it thickens, starts to bubble and the temperature reads 170°F (75°C) on an instant-read thermometer, 6 to 8 minutes. If you don't have a thermometer, cook the curd until it coats the back of a spoon and leaves a distinct trail when you run your finger through it.

Remove the curd from the heat. Add the butter, a few cubes at a time, to the saucepan, waiting for each cube to melt before adding the next, and the curd consistency is smooth. Transfer the curd to the sieve and push it through with a wooden spoon. Allow the curd to cool to room temperature.

Pour the curd into the baked shell and smooth the top with an offset spatula. Cover the tart loosely with tinfoil, being sure not to let the tinfoil touch the curd (plastic wrap will stick to the surface and leave marks). Place the tart in the refrigerator to firm up, about 2 hours.

Decorate the Tart

Place the blueberries in a wreath around the tart. Place the blackberries, strawberries and goldenberries amongst the blueberries. Add the cherries amongst the other fruit. Place the 1-inch (3-cm) pastry flowers decoratively amongst the fruit. If desired, place edible flowers of your choice amongst the fruit. Carefully unmold the completely cooled tart from the tin and serve.

To Make Ahead or Store

The tart is best eaten on the day it is made. Leftovers can be stored, tightly covered in the refrigerator, for up to 2 days.

Note:

Goldenberries are also known as Cape gooseberries or Inca berries. If you can't find them, try substituting golden cherries or any fruit of your choice.

Equipment

9-inch (23-cm) round tart tin with removable bottom, about 1 inch (3 cm) deep

½-inch (13-mm) flower cutter

1-inch (3-cm) flower cutter

Instant-read thermometer

Lime and Matcha Tart with Pretzel Crust

Featured Decoration: Two-Color Swirls

Make the Pretzel Crust

Adjust the oven rack to the lower-middle position and place a baking sheet on it. Preheat the oven to 350°F (175°C).

Place the pretzel sticks and sugar in a food processor bowl and pulse until the pretzel sticks are mostly ground. You should have about 1½ cups (60 g) of pretzel crumbs. Add the melted butter to the processor bowl and pulse eight to ten times to thoroughly combine.

Transfer the mixture to the tart tin and press it evenly into the bottom and up the sides of the tin. Transfer the tin to the preheated baking sheet in the oven and bake for 20 minutes, or until the crumb mixture is set and slightly browned. Remove the tin from the oven and allow the shell to cool to room temperature. Return the baking sheet to the oven, leaving the oven set to 350°F (175°C).

Make the Lime and Matcha Filling

In a medium bowl, whisk together the condensed milk and eggs until blended. Add the lime juice and zest. Whisk again until the mixture thickens and is completely smooth. Set aside.

Measure ½ cup (120 ml) of the lime filling and place it in a small bowl. Add the matcha powder and whisk with a fork until it is completely incorporated. Place the bowls of lime filling and the lime–matcha filling in the refrigerator for 15 minutes to thicken up slightly.

(Continued)

This tart is a match(a) made in heaven. A no-fuss, silky lime and matcha filling with just the right amount of zing teams up with a salty pretzel crust with just the right amount of crunch. The simple swirl design reminds me of swaying garden ferns on an early summer's morning.

Makes one single-crust, 9-inch (23-cm) round tart

3 cups (360 g) pretzel sticks

4 tbsp (50 g) granulated sugar

10 tbsp (140 g) unsalted butter, melted

2 (14-oz [397-g]) cans sweetened condensed milk

2 large eggs, lightly beaten

1 cup (240 ml) freshly squeezed lime juice (7 to 9 limes)

1 tsp freshly grated lime zest

1 tbsp (6 g) matcha powder

Equipment

9-inch (23-cm) round tart tin with removable bottom, about 1 inch (3 cm) deep

Piping bag

½-inch (13-mm) plain piping tip

Wooden skewer

Lime and Matcha Tart with Pretzel Crust (Continued)

Create the Swirl Effect
Remove the lime filling from the refrigerator and pour it into the baked pretzel tart shell. Smooth with an offset spatula.

Place a disposable piping bag fitted with a ½-inch (13-mm) plain tip into a tall glass and fold the piping bag collar down. Bend the piping bag tip upward so the filling doesn't drip out when you fill it. Remove the lime–matcha filling from the refrigerator and spoon it into the piping bag.

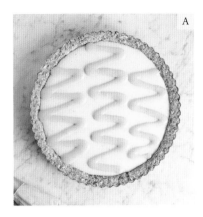

Pipe a zigzag of filling down the left-hand side of the tart. Repeat the zigzag in the middle of the tart and again on the right-hand side of the tart (photo A). Using the thin end of the skewer, and starting in the top left-hand quadrant of the tart, run the skewer in a looping pattern through the zigzags, moving side to side, top to bottom (photo B). Turn the pan a quarter turn clockwise and repeat the same looping motion to create the swirly design (photo C). If you'd like more swirls, continue to rotate the pan, one quarter turn at a time, using the same looping motion, until you achieve your desired effect.

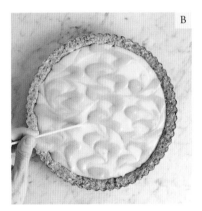

Bake the Tart
Place the tart on the preheated baking sheet in the oven and bake for 18 to 20 minutes, or until the filling is set around the edges but still jiggles slightly in the middle when shaken. Let the tart cool to room temperature and then refrigerate until very firm, approximately 4 hours. Unmold and serve.

To Make Ahead or Store
The tart is best eaten on the day it is made. Leftovers can be stored, tightly covered in the refrigerator, for up to 2 days.

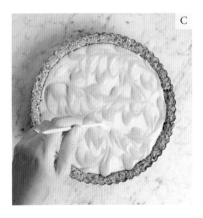

Winter's Evening Mini Tourtières (page 69)

chapter 3

Field and Forest Inspirations

Nature provides a seemingly endless source of inspiration. Often, a long walk in the woods will result in me rushing back to my kitchen to try to re-create, in pastry, the deep crevices of bark on an old oak tree or the shape of the aspen leaves I saw fluttering in the breeze. From stick-to-your-ribs Winter's Evening Mini Tourtières (page 69) decorated with embossed pie dough to camping-inspired Campfire S'mores Tartlets (page 73) and a Walk in the Woods Salted Maple Caramel Apple Pie covered in pastry acorns (page 61), the recipes and decorations in this chapter reflect the beauty of the great outdoors and our place in it.

Chocolate Cream Tart with Pinecones and Needles

Featured Decorations: Chocolate Pine Needles & Chocolate-Almond Pinecones

Make the Crust

Adjust the oven rack to the lower-middle position and preheat the oven to 375°F (190°C).

In a medium bowl, combine the chocolate cookie or chocolate graham cracker crumbs, sugar and ground almonds. Add the melted butter and mix with a fork until thoroughly combined.

Press the mixture evenly across the bottom and up the sides of the tart tin. Transfer the tart tin to the oven and bake for 20 minutes, or until the crumb mixture is set. Cool to room temperature.

Make the Chocolate Cream Filling

In a medium bowl, combine the chopped chocolate, espresso powder, vanilla and salt. In a medium saucepan over medium heat, bring 1 cup (240 ml) of the heavy cream to a bare simmer. Pour the hot cream over the chocolate mixture and let it stand for 1 minute. Whisk until it is smooth. Set the mixture aside to let it cool to room temperature on the counter, stirring occasionally.

Using an electric mixer or hand beaters, whip the remaining 2 cups (480 ml) of cream with the sugar until stiff peaks form. Gently fold the whipped cream into the cooled chocolate mixture until no streaks remain. Pour the chocolate cream into the prepared cooled tart shell and gently smooth with an offset spatula. Refrigerate for 2 hours, or until firm.

Make the Almond Pinecones (see Note)

In a small microwave-safe bowl, combine the chocolate chips, condensed milk, butter and salt. Microwave on high for 30 seconds. Remove the bowl and stir. Repeat this process, using 15-second microwave bursts, stirring each time, until the mixture is melted and completely smooth. Press a piece of plastic wrap directly onto the surface of the mixture and refrigerate for 30 minutes, or until cool and firm.

Line a baking sheet with parchment paper. Using a teaspoon measurement, scoop out nine balls of the chocolate mixture. (You will not use all of the mixture.) In the palm of your hand, roll the scoops into ovals and pinch one end so they resemble pinecone shapes. Place them on the parchment-lined baking sheet.

(Continued)

A lot of my tarts are inspired by nature, and this one is no exception. Because there are three components to this tart—the cream tart, the pinecones and the needles—feel free to tackle this project over 2 days. Both the needles and the pinecones will be happy to hang out in your refrigerator for up to a week. The shell can be made the day before and assembled with the decorations on the day you plan to serve this tart.

Makes one 9-inch (23-cm), single-crust deep-dish tart

Chocolate-Almond Crust

1½ cups (120 g) chocolate cookie crumbs or chocolate graham crackers, finely ground

¼ cup (50 g) granulated sugar

½ cup (56 g) finely ground almonds

½ cup (120 g) unsalted butter, melted

Chocolate Cream Filling

10 oz (284 g) good-quality semisweet chocolate, finely chopped

1 tsp espresso powder

1 tsp pure vanilla extract

Pinch of kosher salt

3 cups (720 ml) heavy cream, chilled, divided

¼ cup (50 g) granulated sugar

Chocolate Cream Tart with Pinecones and Needles (Continued)

Place ½ cup (60 g) of the chocolate candy melts in a small microwave-proof bowl and microwave them for 10 seconds. Stir and repeat this process until the wafers have completely melted.

Use a small paintbrush to cover one end of an almond slice in melted chocolate. Press the chocolate-covered tip of the almond slice against the tip of the pinecone. Repeat with the second almond slice, overlapping the first one slightly. Continue around the oval, moving top to bottom, until the chocolate oval is completely covered in almonds (photo A). Lay the finished almond pinecone on the parchment-lined baking sheet. Repeat this process until you have nine pinecones. Transfer the pinecones, on the baking sheet, to the refrigerator and allow them to chill for 10 minutes, or until firm.

Make the Chocolate Needles
Fit a piping bag with a ⅛-inch (3-mm) plain tip. Line a baking sheet with parchment paper.

Place 1 cup (120 g) of the chocolate candy melts in a small microwave-proof bowl and microwave for 20 seconds. Stir and repeat this process, using 10-second bursts, until the wafers have completely melted and have a honey-like consistency. Transfer the melted chocolate to the piping bag. Pipe thin, straight lines of chocolate onto the parchment paper. Transfer the chocolate lines to the refrigerator on the baking sheet and cool for 10 minutes, or until firm. Using a sharp knife, cut the chocolate lines into ¾-inch (2-cm)-long pieces.

Decorate the Tart
Unmold the tart and place it on a plate. Sprinkle the top of the tart with the chocolate needles. Place the pinecones decoratively on top. Return the tart to the refrigerator and let it set for 2 hours before serving.

To Make Ahead or Store
While the tart is best eaten on the day it is made, the chocolate needles and almond pinecones can be made up to 1 week ahead. The shell can be baked 1 day ahead. The chocolate cream is best made on the day it is to be served.

Note:
If you do not have a microwave, you can use ready-made chocolate or brown fondant (available at most cake supply stores).

Almond Pinecones and Chocolate Needles
¾ cup (128 g) semisweet chocolate chips

⅓ cup (80 ml) condensed milk

1 tbsp (15 g) unsalted butter

Dash of kosher salt

1½ cups (180 g) chocolate candy melts, divided

1 cup (100 g) sliced almonds

Equipment
9-inch (23-cm) round, deep-dish tart tin with removable bottom, 1½ inches (4 cm) deep

Small paintbrush

Piping bag

⅛-inch (3-mm) plain piping tip

A

Walk in the Woods Salted Maple Caramel Apple Pie

Featured Decorations: Pie Dough Acorns & Leaves, Embossed Lattice, Braids

Make the Salted Maple Caramel Sauce

In a small saucepan, combine the maple syrup and brown sugar. Cook over medium heat, stirring constantly, until the sugar has melted. Allow the liquid sugar to boil, swirling the pan occasionally, until the mixture is an amber color and reads 250°F (120°C) on a candy thermometer, about 5 minutes. Keep a close eye on the liquid sugar as it will go from amber to burnt in a few seconds. Reduce the heat to low and add the butter (the mixture will boil up initially so be careful). Continue stirring until the butter is melted and the mixture is smooth.

Add the heavy cream in a steady stream and stir over medium-low heat until thickened, 3 to 5 minutes. Remove the caramel sauce from the heat, add the salt and stir again until the salt has dissolved. Set the sauce aside to cool to room temperature.

Make the Pie Shell

In a small bowl, whisk together the egg and milk to make the egg wash. Set aside.

Cut a piece of parchment paper at least 12 inches (30 cm) long. Flip the pie plate upside down and, using it as a guide, mark a 9-inch (23-cm) circle on the parchment paper. You will use it later to build your lattice.

Remove one disc of the Everyday All-Butter Pie Dough from the refrigerator and roll it out to a 12-inch (30-cm) circle, about ⅛ inch (3 mm) thick. Transfer and fit the pie dough to the pie pan, following the technique in the Lining a Pie Plate or Tin section on pages 170 and 171, and trimming the overhang to ½ inch (13 mm). Place the pie shell in the refrigerator while you make the decorations.

Make the Acorns and Leaves

Line a baking sheet with parchment paper and set aside. Remove the second disc of Everyday All-Butter Pie Dough from the refrigerator. Cut off twelve walnut-sized pieces of dough from the disc and roll each into an oval shape that is approximately ½ x 1 inch (13 mm x 3 cm). Pinch one end of each oval to create the tip of the acorn and flatten out the other end slightly (photo A [page 62]). To make the acorn "hats," on a lightly floured surface, roll out the remainder of the dough disc to a ⅛-inch (3-mm) thickness. Use a ½-inch (13-mm) circle cutter or a piping tip to cut twelve circles. With the back of a knife, create a crisscross design on the top of each circle. Brush the top of each acorn with a small amount of egg wash and then wrap the "hat" around it (photo B [page 62]). Repeat with the remaining acorns. Place the finished acorns on the baking sheet.

(Continued)

I have a weak spot for caramel apples so this pie hits all the right notes for me. Not too sweet. Not too salty. The addition of a little pure maple syrup adds a woodsy flavor to the caramel-soaked apples. And don't even get me started on those adorable little pastry acorns. Seriously, make this!

Makes one double-crust, 9-inch (23-cm) round, deep-dish pie

Salted Maple Caramel Sauce

¼ cup (60 ml) pure maple syrup

½ cup (110 g) dark brown sugar, packed

¼ cup (60 g) unsalted butter, diced

½ cup (120 ml) heavy cream

1 tsp kosher salt

Pie Crust and Decorations

1 large egg

1 tsp milk

3 discs Everyday All-Butter Pie Dough (page 21), chilled

Apple Filling

½ cup (100 g) granulated sugar

1½ tsp (4 g) cinnamon

⅓ cup (42 g) tapioca flour or cornstarch

4 lb (1.8 kg) apples (Gala, Spy, Cortland, Golden Delicious or a mix), cored, peeled and sliced ¼ inch (6 mm) thick

2 tbsp (30 ml) freshly squeezed lemon juice

Walk in the Woods Salted Maple Caramel Apple Pie (Continued)

Cut twelve oak leaves and twelve maple leaves from the same piece of rolled-out dough. If necessary, reroll the scraps. Use the back of a knife or a veining tool to mark veins in the leaves. Place the cutouts on the baking sheet and set aside.

Make the Lattice

Remove the third disc of Everyday All-Butter Pie Dough from the refrigerator and roll it out to a 12 x 14–inch (30 x 36–cm) rectangle, about ¼ inch (6 mm) thick. Cut the dough in half so you have two 7 x 12–inch (18 x 30–cm) pieces. Set one aside. With the woodgrain impression mat (see the Embossing Pie Dough section on page 174 for instructions), emboss one strip of dough. From this embossed piece, cut two 1½ x 12–inch (4 x 30–cm) strips and eight ½ x 12–inch (13-mm x 30-cm) strips. Place the strips on the baking sheet with the leaves and acorns.

From the remaining unembossed pie dough sheet, cut six ½ x 12–inch (13-mm x 30-cm) strips of dough. Make two 3-strand braids, following the directions in the Twist and Braiding Techniques section on page 175. Place them on the baking sheet with the other decorations and transfer the baking sheet to the refrigerator to chill for 5 minutes.

Place the parchment paper with the outline of the pie pan you made earlier on a flat surface, marked side down, but ensuring that you can still see the outline through it.

Following the latticing technique outlined in the Latticing a Pie section on pages 177 and 178, and working from left to right on the parchment outline, lay the pie dough strips in the following order (use the photo for reference on spacing): a set of embossed ½-inch (13-mm) strips (side by side), one 1½-inch (4-cm) embossed strip, one braid and two embossed ½-inch (13-mm) strips (side by side). Turn the parchment a quarter turn, and weave the remaining strips in the same order, left to right, so they intersect with your first set of strips.

Slide the parchment paper, with the lattice on it, onto a baking sheet and transfer it to the freezer for 15 minutes.

Make the Apple Filling

In a small bowl, whisk together the sugar, cinnamon and tapioca flour or cornstarch. In a large bowl, combine the apples and lemon juice. Sprinkle the sugar/spice mixture over the apples and toss to combine. Set aside.

(Continued)

Equipment

Candy thermometer

9-inch (23-cm) round deep-dish pie plate, 2 inches (5 cm) deep

½-inch (13-mm) circle cutter

2-inch (5-cm) oak leaf cutter

2-inch (5-cm) maple leaf cutter

Veining tool, optional

Woodgrain impression mat

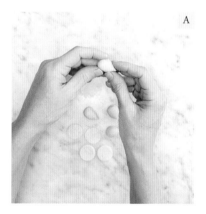

A

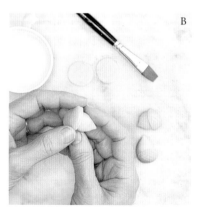

B

Walk in the Woods Salted Maple Caramel Apple Pie (Continued)

Assemble the Pie

Remove the chilled pie shell from the refrigerator. Add half of the apple filling to the pie shell, packing the fruit as tightly as possible. Drizzle ¼ cup (60 ml) of the maple caramel sauce over the apples. Add the remaining apple pie filling and drizzle with another ¼ cup (60 ml) of the maple caramel sauce.

Brush the pie shell edges with the egg wash. Remove the lattice top from the freezer. Slide a pizza lifter or large spatula under the lattice and gently move it onto the prepared pie shell. Center the design on the pie top. The lattice top will be quite stiff, making it easy to adjust. When you are happy with the placement, and the lattice strips have softened a bit, trim the edges of the lattice to ¼ inch (6 mm), and tuck it neatly over and under the bottom dough overhang to seal. Trim the excess dough.

Brush the lattice with egg wash. Arrange the leaves decoratively around the border of the lattice. Bend and turn the leaves to give them dimension. Tuck some of the pie dough acorns between the leaves and place others on top of the leaves. With leftover scraps of dough, roll some additional small balls of pie dough to create small berries and sprinkle these among the leaves and acorns.

Transfer the pie to the freezer for 30 minutes. While waiting, adjust the oven rack to the lower-middle position and place a baking sheet on it. Preheat the oven to 425°F (220°C).

Bake the Pie

Egg wash the decorations on top of the pie. Transfer the pie to the preheated baking sheet in the oven and bake for 15 minutes at 425°F (220°C). Turn the temperature down to 375°F (190°C) and bake for another 50 to 60 minutes, or until the pastry is golden brown and the filling is bubbling in the center of the pie. Remove the pie from the oven and allow it to set for at least 3 hours before serving.

To Make Ahead or Store

The pie can be baked 1 day ahead and stored at room temperature, loosely covered. Leftover pie can be covered and stored at room temperature for up to 2 days.

The unbaked pie may be frozen, egg washed and double wrapped, for up to 3 months. It must be baked from frozen. You may need to add an additional 10 to 15 minutes to the baking time for frozen pies.

Blistered Tomato Galette

Featured Decoration: Ruffled Phyllo

Make the Basil Pesto

In a small skillet, toast ⅓ cup (45 g) of the pine nuts over medium-low heat for 2 to 3 minutes, shaking the pan regularly, until the pine nuts are evenly browned. Remove the skillet from the heat and transfer the pine nuts to the bowl of a food processor.

Add the basil leaves, Parmesan cheese, lemon juice, garlic and salt to the food processor bowl. Pulse the ingredients three to four times to roughly combine. With the food processor running, slowly drizzle ½ cup (120 ml) of the olive oil through the tube into the mixture. Continue processing until the pesto is well blended but still has some texture, approximately 1 to 2 minutes, scraping down the bowl as necessary.

Blister the Tomatoes

Using a sharp knife or skewer, poke a hole in the top or side of each tomato. In a heavy skillet over a medium-high heat, warm 2 tablespoons (30 ml) of the olive oil until it starts to shimmer. Turn the heat down to medium. Add the tomatoes and give the skillet a shake to coat them in oil. Cook them, undisturbed, for 1 to 2 minutes, or until they start to blister and begin to break down. Shake the pan again and continue cooking until all sides are blistered, an additional 2 to 3 minutes. Remove the tomatoes from the heat and add salt and pepper to taste.

Assemble the Galette

Adjust the oven rack to the middle position. Preheat the oven to 400°F (205°C). Trim the phyllo sheets to 14 x 14 inches (36 x 36 cm). Line a baking sheet with parchment paper. Place one sheet of phyllo on the parchment paper, covering the rest with plastic wrap or wax paper and then a damp towel to prevent the phyllo from drying out as you work.

Using a pastry brush, brush the phyllo sheet with the melted butter. Turn the baking sheet clockwise a one-eighth turn. Place another sheet of phyllo, straight up and down, over the first buttered sheet and brush the second sheet with butter. Continue this process for the remaining sheets of phyllo, rotating a one-eighth turn and brushing the sheet with butter each time.

Spoon the ricotta into the center of the phyllo sheet base and spread thickly to form a 10-inch (25-cm) circle. Drizzle ⅓ cup (82 g) of the pesto over the ricotta, reserving any extra for another use.

(Continued)

This galette is a true natural beauty, featuring a gorgeous bounty of tomatoes in all shapes, sizes and colors, and lemony ricotta and basil pesto nestled in a buttery, ruffled phyllo border. Include as many tomato colors and shapes as you can find but don't spend too much time fussing. This galette already has what it takes to stand out from the crowd.

Makes one 9-inch (23-cm) freeform galette

⅓ cup + ¼ cup (79 g) pine nuts, divided

2 cups (50 g) packed fresh basil leaves

½ cup (40 g) freshly grated Parmesan cheese

1 tbsp (15 ml) lemon juice

1 clove garlic, chopped

½ tsp kosher salt

½ cup + 2 tbsp (150 ml) extra-virgin olive oil, divided

2 cups (300 g) cherry tomatoes, various sizes, shapes and colors (such as an heirloom mix)

Kosher salt and pepper, to taste

8 fresh phyllo pastry sheets, or frozen and thawed, at least 16 x 14 inches (41 x 36 cm)

¼ cup (60 g) unsalted butter, melted

1 cup (250 g) ricotta cheese, drained of excess moisture

1 tsp thyme, chopped

Blistered Tomato Galette (Continued)

Decoratively nestle the tomatoes on top of the ricotta and pesto mixture, paying attention to balancing the colors and sizes of tomatoes.

Lift one edge of the phyllo border and fold it inward, squeezing the phyllo gently in your hand to create a ruffled border around the ricotta and pesto. Continue working your way around the galette until the tomatoes and filling are completely surrounded by the phyllo. Sprinkle the chopped thyme and the remaining ¼ cup (34 g) of pine nuts over the tomatoes.

Brush the border gently with any remaining melted butter. Place the galette in the oven and bake for 25 to 30 minutes, or until the tomatoes have blistered and the phyllo is a deep golden brown.

Allow the galette to cool for 10 minutes before serving.

To Make Ahead or Store
The galette is best served within 3 hours of baking (it tends to get a bit soggy after that). You can rewarm and crisp up the galette by placing it on a baking sheet in a preheated 350°F (175°C) oven for 10 minutes.

Winter's Evening Mini Tourtières

Featured Decorations: Embossed Pastry Shell, Pie Dough Wreath, Braids

Make the Filling

In a large, heavy skillet over medium heat, sauté the bacon until it is crisp. Transfer the bacon to a small bowl, leaving the fat that has rendered in the skillet. Over medium heat, sauté the garlic and onion in the fat, stirring often, until the onion has softened, about 5 minutes. Add the mushrooms to the mixture and cook until all the liquid has evaporated, 5 to 7 minutes. Add the wine, scraping up any brown bits on the bottom of the skillet. Bring the mixture to a boil and stir until the liquid has almost completely evaporated, about 3 minutes.

Add the salt, pepper, cinnamon, cloves and nutmeg to the skillet. Stir for 1 minute to allow the spices to warm and become fragrant. Add the ground pork and beef and continue to cook, breaking up any lumps, until the meat is no longer pink, 5 to 7 minutes. Add the cooked bacon back in along with the grated potato and continue cooking until the potato begins to soften, about 5 minutes. Add the maple syrup to the mixture and stir to combine. Remove the filling from the heat and allow the mixture to cool to room temperature.

Decorate the Mini Tourtières

Line two baking sheets with parchment paper and set aside.

Remove one disc of Savory Pie Dough from the refrigerator. On a lightly floured surface, roll the dough out to a 10-inch (25-cm) square. Cut twelve 1-inch (3-cm) maple leaves and twelve 1½-inch (4-cm) maple leaves and add them to one of the baking sheets.

Rerolling the scraps if necessary, cut eight ¼ x 6–inch (6-mm x 15-cm) dough strips. From these, create four 2-strand braids, following the directions in the Twist and Braiding Techniques section on pages 175 and 176. Add the braids to the baking sheet with the leaves and transfer to the refrigerator.

(Continued)

These hearty and filling French-Canadian meat pies originated in the province of Quebec where they remain a traditional part of Christmas and New Year's celebrations. This mini version of the classic pie pays tribute to the Great Northern outdoors with tree bark–embossed pastry and leaf wreaths. The tourtières, featuring two types of meats, smoky bacon and the caramel flavor of maple syrup, are guaranteed to stick to your ribs on the coldest of days.

Makes four double-crust, 4-inch (10-cm)-tourtières

4 slices bacon, roughly chopped

3 garlic cloves, minced

1 large onion, finely chopped (1½ cups [240 g])

8 brown mushrooms, finely chopped

½ cup (120 ml) dry white wine

1 tsp kosher salt

½ tsp pepper

½ tsp cinnamon

⅛ tsp ground cloves

⅛ tsp ground nutmeg

1 lb (454 g) ground pork

½ lb (227 g) ground beef

1 russet potato, peeled and grated (approximately ¾ cup [115 g])

2 tbsp (30 ml) maple syrup

3 discs Savory Pie Dough (page 21), chilled

1 large egg

1 tsp milk

Winter's Evening Mini Tourtières (Continued)

Remove the second disc of Savory Pie Dough from the refrigerator. Add any scraps from the first disc of dough to the bottom of this disc. On a lightly floured surface, roll it out to a 12-inch (30-cm) square, approximately ¼ inch (6 mm) thick. Emboss the dough with a woodgrain impression mat, following the technique in the Embossing Pie Dough section on page 174 (photo A). Using a sharp knife and a ruler, cut four 2½ x 12–inch (6.5 x 30–cm) strips across the grain of the woodgrain impression (photo B). Place the embossed strips on the second prepared baking sheet.

Remove the third disc of Savory Pie Dough from the refrigerator. Add any dough scraps from the second disc of dough to the bottom of this disc. On a lightly floured surface, roll the dough out to a 12-inch (30-cm) square. Using your impression mat and a rolling pin, emboss a distinct woodgrain impression across the pie dough. Using the top of the springform pan as a guide, cut eight 4-inch (10-cm) circles and place them on the baking sheet with the woodgrain dough strips. Return the decorations to the refrigerator until the pie dough firms up, about 10 minutes. Save the leftover scraps of dough for assembly of the tourtières.

Assemble the Tourtières

In a small bowl, whisk together the egg and milk to make the egg wash. Set aside.

Remove the two baking sheets of decorations from the refrigerator. Gently place one of the embossed strips of dough inside one of the springform pans, ensuring that the impression side faces outward (so it will show when you release it from the springform). Try to fit the strip snugly without pressing on the embossed dough as this can affect the design.

Leaving a ¼-inch (6-mm) overlap where the two ends meet, add a little egg wash and gently press down on the seam to ensure it is sealed. Trim away any excess dough. Brush a small amount of egg wash around the inside bottom border. Place a 4-inch (10-cm) dough circle at the bottom of the pan, with the woodgrain facing down. Use your fingers to push the circle out slightly so it overlaps with the side strip of dough. Press to seal the base to the sides (photo C [page 71]). With a sharp knife, trim away any excess dough hanging above the top of the springform pan. Repeat for the other three springform pans. Place the four lined springform pans in the freezer for 10 minutes to firm up.

Equipment

1-inch (3-cm) maple leaf cutter

1½-inch (4-cm) maple leaf cutter

Woodgrain impression mat

Ruler

Four 4 x 2–inch (10 x 5–cm) springform pans with removable bottoms

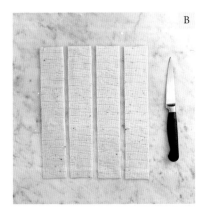

Remove the lined springform pans from the freezer and divide the tourtière filling evenly among them. The filling should be flush to the top of the pans. Brush a small amount of egg wash around the dough edges, and place the remaining embossed dough circles on top (photo D).

Using your fingers, press down and around the edges to ensure that the top seals to the dough edges. Trim away any excess. Brush with more egg wash. Place an entwined dough strip around the edge of one half of each tourtière top. On the other side, place the maple leaves in a curved design, alternating the two sizes, and twisting and bending the leaves to create a realistic look (photo E). To give the tourtières more dimension, place small balls of dough underneath the leaves to help keep them "propped up" in the oven. Brush the entwined strips and the leaves with egg wash and place the tourtières in the freezer for 30 minutes.

In the meantime, adjust the oven rack to the lower–middle position and place a baking sheet on it. Preheat the oven to 425°F (220°C).

Bake the Tourtières
When the pies have chilled, place them in the oven on the preheated baking sheet and bake them for 10 minutes. Reduce the temperature to 375°F (190°C) and continue to bake for another 30 to 35 minutes, or until the pastry is golden brown. Allow the pies to cool for at least 30 minutes before releasing them from the springform pans and serving.

To Make Ahead or Store
The tourtière filling and/or complete pies can be made/baked up to 2 days ahead and stored, tightly wrapped in the refrigerator. Leftovers can be covered and stored in the refrigerator for up to 2 days.

The unbaked tourtières can be frozen, egg washed and double wrapped, for up to 3 months, and then baked from frozen. You may need to add an additional 10 to 15 minutes to the baking time for frozen pies.

See photo on page 56.

Campfire S'mores Tartlets

Featured Decorations: Chocolate & Marshmallow Campfires

Make the Graham Cracker Tarts

Place the graham cracker crumbs in a medium bowl. Pour the melted butter over them and stir until fully incorporated. Evenly divide the mixture among six tartlet tins or silicone molds, or an 8-inch (20-cm) tart tin if using. Use the bottom of a straight-sided juice glass or a small measuring cup to press the mixture firmly into the sides and bottom of the tins. Place the shells on a baking sheet and transfer to the refrigerator to chill while you prepare the filling.

Make the Chocolate Ganache Filling

Adjust the oven rack to the lower-middle position and preheat the oven to 350°F (175°C). Place the chopped chocolate in a heatproof bowl and set aside. In a small saucepan, heat the heavy cream over medium heat until it begins to bubble around the edges, being sure to not let it boil. Pour the hot cream over the chopped chocolate and cover the bowl with a plate or plastic wrap. Let the mixture stand, without stirring, for 5 minutes, then whisk it until it is thick and glossy, 1 to 2 minutes. Add the salt and the beaten egg and whisk again until all the ingredients are fully incorporated.

Remove the shells from the refrigerator. Divide the ganache mixture evenly among the shells. Transfer the tartlets, on the baking sheet, to the oven and bake for 15 to 17 minutes for the tartlets or 25 to 30 minutes for the tart, or until the outer edge of the filling is set but the center still wobbles slightly when shaken. Cool slightly on a cooling rack before proceeding, about 10 minutes.

Decorate the S'mores Tartlets

Set the oven to broil, leaving the oven rack in the lower-middle position. Top each tartlet with eleven mini-marshmallows, arranging them in a circle around the edge of the chocolate filling. Place the tartlets back on the baking sheet, and transfer them to the oven for approximately 1 to 2 minutes, or until the marshmallows are golden brown. Watch them carefully to ensure that the marshmallows do not burn (it can happen very quickly!). Remove the tartlets from the oven and allow them to cool to room temperature, then place them in the freezer for 10 minutes.

When chilled, carefully remove the tarts from their tins or silicone molds. To create the "firewood," break the Pocky sticks into 2-inch (5-cm) pieces (you should have 36 pieces). Working just inside the marshmallow circle, place one end of a Pocky stick piece into the ganache. Directly across from it, place another Pocky piece and lean the two inward, up against each other, to form a tepee. Add four more sticks around each tartlet, leaning them up against each other. Serve at room temperature.

To Make Ahead or Store

The tarts can be baked 1 day ahead and stored, tightly wrapped, in the refrigerator overnight. Leftovers can be stored, covered in the refrigerator, for up to 2 days.

The idea for these mini s'mores tartlets came from summer camping trips spent around the campfire, engaged in a friendly competition over who could make the perfect s'mores. You know the ones . . . crispy and warm graham crackers on the outside with the perfect balance of melty marshmallow and chocolate on the inside. If you can't find a campfire to join, these delicious treats are the next best thing.

Makes six 3-inch (8-cm) round tartlets or one 8-inch (20-cm) tart

1½ cups (120 g) graham cracker crumbs (10 to 15 graham crackers)

½ cup (120 g) unsalted butter, melted

8 oz (227 g) good-quality semisweet dark chocolate, chopped

1 cup (240 ml) heavy cream

Pinch of kosher salt

1 large egg, lightly beaten

66 mini-marshmallows

12 Pocky chocolate sticks, After Eight mint sticks or similar

Equipment

Six 3-inch (8-cm) tartlet tins or silicone molds *or* one 8-inch (20-cm) round tart tin

Harvest Time Concord Grape Pie

Featured Decorations: Pie Dough Leaves & Grapes

Prepare the Pie Shell

Roll out one disc of the Everyday All-Butter Pie Dough to a 12-inch (30-cm) circle. Transfer and fit the pie dough to the pie pan, following the technique in the Lining a Pie Plate or Tin on pages 170 and 171, and trimming the overhang to ½ inch (13 mm). Transfer the plate to the refrigerator while you make the filling. Set the leftover scraps of dough aside.

Make the Filling

Using your fingers, squeeze the grape pulp from their skins (it's easier than it sounds, I promise) into a medium-sized saucepan. Place the skins in a separate, medium bowl and set aside. Bring the pulp to a simmer over medium-low heat, stirring often, until the seeds separate and the pulp breaks down to release its juices, 8 to 10 minutes. Place a fine sieve over the bowl of grape skins and strain the pulp from the saucepan into the bowl, using the back of a wooden spoon to push as much pulp as possible through the sieve. Discard the solids.

In a small bowl, toss the sugar, cornstarch or tapioca starch and salt together. Add it to the grape mixture in the bowl and stir to combine.

Transfer the grape mixture back to the saucepan. On medium-low heat, stir the mixture until it bubbles and thickens, 3 to 5 minutes. Set the mixture aside to cool.

Make the Grape Leaves

In a small bowl, whisk together the egg and milk to make the egg wash. Set aside.

Line a baking sheet with parchment paper and set aside.

Roll out the second disc of Everyday All-Butter Pie Dough to a 12-inch (30-cm) square. Using the three maple leaf cutters, cut six 3-inch (8-cm) maple leaves, eight 2-inch (5-cm) maple leaves and eight 1½-inch (4-cm) maple leaves and place them on the baking sheet. Using the back of a sharp knife or a veining tool, vein all the leaves (photo A [page 76]). Egg wash the leaves and transfer the baking sheet to the refrigerator. Gather the leftover dough scraps and set aside with the scraps from the pie shell.

(Continued)

The unique, mellow flavor of Concord Grape Pie lies somewhere between a cherry and a blueberry pie with none of the tartness of the uncooked grape. While these dusky blue beauties are only available for a short time during fall harvest season in wine regions, if you can get your hands on some, make batches of filling to freeze for use in your pies year round. They are that good. Maple leaf cutters mimic the look of grape leaves here while rolled balls of dough are used to create a bountiful grape harvest.

Makes one double-crust, 9-inch (23-cm) pie

2 discs Everyday All-Butter Pie Dough (page 21)

2 lb (907 g) Concord grapes, stemmed

¾ cup (150 g) sugar

4 tbsp (32 g) cornstarch or tapioca flour

Pinch of kosher salt

1 large egg

1 tsp milk

Equipment

9-inch (23-cm) round pie plate, about 1¼ inches (3.5 cm) deep

3-inch (8-cm) maple leaf cutter

2-inch (5-cm) maple leaf cutter

1½-inch (4-cm) maple leaf cutter

Veining tool, optional

Wooden skewer

Harvest Time Concord Grape Pie (Continued)

Assemble the Pie

Adjust the oven rack to the lower-middle position and place a baking sheet on it. Preheat the oven to 425°F (220°C). Remove the pie shell from the refrigerator and fill it with the cooled grape mixture. Place the leaves decoratively over the pie filling, arching and bending them to give them a realistic look (photo B).

Make the Grape Clusters and Tendrils

Using the leftover dough you set aside, roll small balls of dough in varying sizes to create the grape clusters. Place the grapes in bunches on and among the leaves in a reverse pyramid shape. To make the tendrils, pull off six to eight small pieces of leftover dough, each about the size of a grape. With your fingers, roll out each piece into a long, thin strand. Wind the strands around a skewer and place on a parchment-lined baking sheet in the freezer for 5 minutes. Slide the tendrils off the skewers and place decoratively at the top of the grape clusters (photo C). Transfer the pie to the freezer for 30 minutes.

Bake the Pie

Brush the grape clusters gently with some of the remaining egg wash. Transfer the pie to the baking sheet in the preheated oven. Bake for 15 minutes. Turn the heat down to 375°F (190°C). Bake for another 45 to 55 minutes until the pie is golden brown and the filling is bubbling up in the center. Let the pie cool for at least 3 hours before serving to ensure it is completely set.

To Make Ahead or Store

The pie can be baked up to 1 day ahead and stored, loosely wrapped, at room temperature. Leftovers can be covered and stored at room temperature for up to 3 days.

The unbaked pie can be frozen, egg washed and double wrapped, for up to 3 months, and then baked from frozen. You may need to add an additional 10 to 15 minutes to the baking time for frozen pies.

See baked photo on page 2.

Turning Leaves Bacon, Onion and Mushroom Quiche

Featured Decorations: Mottled Pie Dough, Pie Dough Leaves

Prepare the Shell

Adjust the oven rack to the middle position. Preheat the oven to 350°F (175°C).

Remove the disc of Savory Pie Dough from the refrigerator. On a lightly floured surface, roll it out to a 12-inch (30-cm) circle. Line the tart tin with the pie dough, following the technique in the Lining a Pie Plate or Tin section on pages 170 and 171, and leaving a 1-inch (3-cm) overhang beyond the rim of the tart tin. Place the lined shell in the freezer for 30 minutes.

Make the Mottled Leaves

Line a baking sheet with parchment paper and set aside. Remove the disc of Golden Yellow Turmeric Pie Dough from the refrigerator. Cut off six walnut-sized pieces of dough from the disc and set aside. Return the rest of the disc to the refrigerator for another use.

Remove the disc of Forest Green Spinach Pie Dough from the refrigerator. Cut the disc of dough into six even pieces and place on a lightly floured surface. Add the six walnut-sized pieces of turmeric dough and leave the pie dough to warm for about 10 minutes. With your hands, gently push the spinach and turmeric dough together into one ball (photo A).

(Continued)

A

This gorgeous quiche celebrates the turning of the leaves and the shift to cooler fall days. I'm not sure what to love more—the creamy egg custard with loads of aged cheddar, smoky bacon, onions and mushrooms or the savory crust and tasty spinach- and turmeric-mottled pastry leaves. Either way, I'm digging in.

Makes one 9-inch (23-cm) round tart

1 disc Savory Pie Dough (page 21)

1 disc Golden Yellow Turmeric Pie Dough (page 27)

1 disc Forest Green Spinach Pie Dough (page 27)

1 red onion, whole, peeled

2 tbsp (30 ml) olive oil, divided

1 cup (85 g) mushrooms, thinly sliced

10 whole cherry tomatoes, assorted colors

5 slices bacon

4 large eggs

1¼ cups (300 ml) heavy cream

Pinch ground nutmeg

½ tsp kosher salt

1 cup (113 g) aged cheddar cheese, shredded

Equipment

9-inch (23-cm) round tart tin with removable bottom, about 1 inch (3 cm) deep

Assorted leaf cutters, 1½- or 2-inch (4- or 5-cm) sizes

Turning Leaves Bacon, Onion and Mushroom Quiche (Continued)

On a lightly floured surface, roll the dough out to a 12-inch (30-cm) circle of mottled pie dough (photo B). Using the leaf cutters, cut 36 leaves. Set them on the prepared baking sheet and transfer to the refrigerator.

Bake the Shell
Remove the shell from the freezer and fully blind bake it following the instructions in the Partial and Full Blind Baking section on pages 172 and 173. After baking, allow the shell to cool slightly, then trim the excess pie dough with a sharp knife.

Prepare the Vegetables and Bacon
Cut the onion into ¼-inch (6-mm) wedges from the root to the stem. In a medium skillet on medium heat, heat 1 tablespoon (15 ml) of the olive oil. Sauté the onion wedges, shaking the pan to keep the onions from sticking, until they begin to brown, about 5 minutes. Transfer the onions to a medium bowl.

Add the mushrooms to the same skillet and sauté until tender and any liquid has absorbed, about 3 minutes. Add them to the bowl with the onions. Add another tablespoon (15 ml) of the olive oil to the skillet and sauté the tomatoes until they start to blister, about 5 minutes. Add the tomatoes to the bowl with the onions and mushrooms.

In the same skillet, over medium-low heat, fry the bacon until it is crisp. Drain on paper towels and crumble. Set aside to cool.

Make the Custard
In a medium bowl, whisk together the eggs, heavy cream, nutmeg and salt. Stir in the shredded cheese. Set aside.

Assemble the Quiche
Place the baked shell on a rimmed cookie sheet. Place half of the onion, tomato and mushroom mixture at the bottom of the baked shell. Pour the egg/cheese mixture over it. Place the remaining onions, mushrooms and tomatoes on top of the custard (don't worry if they sink a little). Sprinkle the quiche with the crumbled bacon. Do not add the leaves yet.

Bake the Quiche
Carefully transfer the cookie sheet with the quiche on it to the oven. Bake the quiche for 15 minutes, or until the custard just starts to set around the edges. Remove the quiche from the oven and add the pie dough leaves in a wreath design around the outer edge of the pie (photo C). Return the quiche to the oven and continue to bake for another 30 minutes, or until the custard is just set in the middle. Unmold the quiche from the tin and serve warm or at room temperature.

To Make Ahead or Store
The quiche is best served the day it is made. Leftovers can be stored in the refrigerator for up to 3 days.

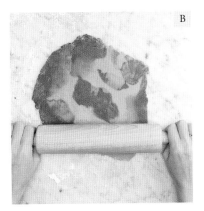

Roasted Vegetable Pithivier (page 93)

chapter 4

Modern Motifs

The designs in this chapter take their cues from modern design across the twentieth century, from contemporary swirls (Starry Night Vegetable Tart, page 83) and concentric circles (Mid-Century Modern Lemon Meringue Tart, page 84) to retro colors (Retro Baked Alaska Tartlets, page 90) and vintage patterns (Roasted Vegetable Pithivier on page 93 and Tumbling Diamonds Blueberry-Lemon Pie on page 96). Don't be afraid to change up the fillings for any of these pies to make your own modern classic.

Starry Night Vegetable Tart

Featured Decoration: Vegetable Spirals

Make the Tart Shell
Adjust the oven rack to the lower-middle position and place a baking sheet on it. Preheat the oven to 375°F (190°C). Remove the Savory Pie Dough disc from the refrigerator. On a lightly floured surface, roll it into an 11 x 14–inch (28 x 36–cm) rectangle. Fit the dough to the tart tin following the directions in the Lining a Pie Plate or Tin section on pages 170 and 171 and leaving a 1-inch (3-cm) overhang. Fully blind bake the pie shell following the directions in the Partial and Full Blind Baking section on pages 172 and 173. After baking, allow the shell to cool slightly, then trim away the excess pie dough with a sharp knife. Set aside.

Make the Filling
In a small bowl, mix the sour cream, pesto and thyme.

Make the Spirals
Using a vegetable peeler, peel the carrots, zucchini and squash in lengthwise strips, placing them on paper towels as you go to absorb any water. Transfer the vegetable strips to a bowl and add the olive oil, salt and pepper. Use your hands to mix gently, being sure to cover the vegetables evenly with the oil.

With your fingers, roll one strip of vegetable tightly into a spiral. Add another strip of vegetable to the end and wrap it around the first strip. Create a series of concentric spirals, using combinations of vegetables and colors, and creating various sizes. The number of spirals that you have will depend on the size you make each spiral.

Assemble the Tart
Reduce the oven temperature to 350°F (175°C). Put the baking sheet back in the oven to preheat. Spread the sour cream/pesto filling evenly on the bottom of the baked tart shell. Place the spirals on top of the filling, making more spirals if necessary to fill in any gaps.

Bake the Tart
Transfer the tart to the preheated baking sheet in the oven. Bake for 45 to 50 minutes, or until the vegetables are tender when pierced with a sharp knife. Allow the tart to cool for 15 minutes. Unmold the tart from the tin and place on a serving platter. Sprinkle with the thyme sprigs and serve.

To Make Ahead or Store
The tart is best served the day it is made. Leftovers can be stored in the refrigerator for up to 3 days.

This hypnotic tart showcases summer vegetables at their best nestled in a pesto base with a flaky tart shell. When my brother-in-law saw it, he insisted that I name it after Vincent van Gogh's painting, The Starry Night. *Who am I to argue with that? This tart is best served warm or at room temperature on the day it's made.*

Makes one 8 x 11-inch (20 x 28-cm) tart

1 disc Savory Pie Dough (page 21), chilled

½ cup (115 g) sour cream

3 tbsp (48 g) homemade or store-bought pesto

1 tsp thyme, finely chopped, plus several sprigs for garnish

6 heirloom carrots, assorted colors if available, scrubbed and trimmed

3 green zucchini

3 yellow squash

1 tbsp (15 ml) olive oil

1 tsp kosher salt

½ tsp pepper

Equipment
8 x 11–inch (20 x 28–cm) tart tin with removable bottom, about 1 inch (3 cm) deep

Mid-Century Modern Lemon Meringue Tart

Featured Decoration: Meringue Circles

Make the Tart Shell

Adjust the oven rack to the lower-middle position and preheat the oven to 350°F (175°C). Roll out the disc of Sweet Tart Dough on a lightly floured surface into a 12-inch (30-cm) circle. Carefully transfer the dough to the tart tin, following the directions in the Lining a Pie Plate or Tin section on pages 170 and 171 and leaving a 1-inch (3-cm) overhang. Fully blind bake the tart shell following the directions in the Partial and Full Blind Baking section on pages 172 and 173. After baking, allow the shell to cool slightly, then trim away the excess pie dough with a sharp knife.

Make the Lemon Curd

Place a sieve over a medium-sized bowl and set aside. In a nonreactive medium saucepan, whisk the lemon juice, lemon zest, granulated sugar, salt and whole eggs until well blended. Heat the mixture over medium-low heat, whisking constantly, until the mixture thickens, starts to bubble and the temperature reads 170°F (75°C) on an instant-read thermometer, 8 to 10 minutes. If you don't have a thermometer, cook until the mixture is glossy and coats the back of a spoon, and leaves a distinct trail when you run your finger through it.

Remove the curd from the heat. Add the butter, a few cubes at a time, and whisk until completely melted and the consistency of the curd is smooth. Pour the curd through the sieve into the pastry shell and allow it to cool to room temperature. Cover the tart with plastic wrap and place it in the refrigerator to firm up, about 2 hours.

Make the Meringue

Using a hand mixer, or in the bowl of a stand mixer fitted with a whisk attachment, beat the egg whites, cream of tartar and salt on medium speed until soft peaks form, about 2 minutes. Add the sugar, about a tablespoon (14 g) at a time, beating thoroughly between additions. After all the sugar has been added, continue beating until the meringue is stiff and shiny and the sugar has completely dissolved, 7 to 10 minutes. To test whether the sugar has dissolved, rub a bit of meringue between your fingers. If the meringue feels gritty, continue beating until the mixture feels smooth.

(Continued)

I have a bit of an obsession with mid-century modern design. Its organic curves, clean lines and cool vibes just make my heart go pitter-patter. This pie is a riff on mid-century modern style with meringue concentric circles taking the place of the traditional swirl. If you're a lover of meringue, feel free to add more concentric circles or make them as big or small as you like. Like the era itself, there are no design limitations here.

Makes one single-crust, 9-inch (23-cm) round tart

1 disc Sweet Tart Dough (page 24)

½ cup (120 ml) fresh lemon juice

2 tsp (4 g) lemon zest, finely grated

¾ cup (150 g) granulated sugar

⅛ tsp kosher salt

3 large eggs

½ cup (120 g) unsalted butter, cut into ½-inch (13-mm) cubes

2 large egg whites

¼ tsp cream of tartar

Pinch of salt

⅔ cup (150 g) superfine sugar (see Note)

Equipment

9-inch (23-cm) round tart tin with removable bottom, about 1 inch (3 cm) deep

Instant-read thermometer

½-inch (13-mm) and ¼-inch (6-mm) plain pastry tips

Piping bags

Kitchen blowtorch, optional

Mid-Century Modern Lemon Meringue Tart (Continued)

Decorate the Tart

Fit one disposable piping bag with a ½-inch (13-mm) plain tip and the other with a ¼-inch (6-mm) round tip. Divide the meringue mixture between the two bags. To create the look of concentric circles, hold the piping tip about ½ inch (13 mm) over the curd. Squeeze the meringue in the piping bag to create a dome of meringue on the curd. Keeping the tip centered, and continuing to apply pressure, slowly lift the piping bag, then release pressure and lift away.

To brown the meringue, use a kitchen blowtorch, or place the pie in a 550°F (290°C) oven for 5 minutes, or until it is nicely browned, watching it very carefully as it will burn quickly. Return the pie to the refrigerator for 2 to 3 hours to cool before serving.

To Make Ahead or Store

The lemon curd can be made up to 3 days ahead and stored in the refrigerator. The shell can be made 1 day ahead and stored, at room temperature, in an airtight container. Assemble on the day the tart is to be eaten.

Note:

You can make your own superfine sugar by processing granulated sugar in a food processor for 2 to 3 minutes.

Blueberry and Raspberry Curd Spheres Tart

Featured Decoration: Curd Spheres

Prepare the Shell

Adjust the oven rack to the lower-middle position and preheat the oven to 375°F (190°C). Roll out the Sweet Tart Dough on a lightly floured surface into a 7 x 16–inch (18 x 41–cm) rectangle, about ⅛ inch (3 mm) thick. Fit the dough to the tart tin following the directions in the Lining a Pie Plate or Tin section on pages 170 and 171, and leaving a 1-inch (3-cm) overhang. Follow the instructions for a full blind bake in the Partial and Full Blind Baking section on pages 172 and 173. After baking, allow the shell to cool slightly, then trim the excess pie dough with a sharp knife.

Make the Blueberry Curd

Place 2 tablespoons (30 ml) of the cold water in a medium bowl. Sprinkle 1 teaspoon of the gelatin over the water. Once the gelatin has bloomed, about 5 minutes, place 2 tablespoons (28 g) of the butter on top of the gelatin. Set a sieve over the bowl and set aside.

In a medium saucepan, whisk two eggs with ½ cup (100 g) of the sugar until thoroughly combined. Add the 12 ounces (340 g) of the fresh or frozen blueberries (including juices if using frozen blueberries) and ¼ cup (60 ml) of the lemon juice. Heat the mixture on a medium-low setting, stirring constantly, until the blueberries have broken down and one or two bubbles burst through the surface of the curd (about 10 minutes) and the curd thickens (it should coat the back of a spoon). Immediately remove the saucepan from the heat and pour the mixture through the sieve and over the gelatin. Press on the solids to get as much blueberry mixture through as possible. Remove the sieve and discard the solids.

Whisk the blueberry–gelatin–butter mixture for 1 minute to ensure all the gelatin is dissolved.

Pour the blueberry curd into three of the 1½-inch (4-cm) sphere cavities and six of the 1-inch (3-cm) sphere cavities and level the tops with an offset spatula. Set the sphere mold trays aside. Pour the remainder of the blueberry curd into the cooled tart shell. Place the curd-filled tart in the refrigerator to firm up, about 2 hours.

(Continued)

With its jewel-tone curd semi-spheres, this impressive dessert has a big wow factor yet is surprisingly easy to pull together. The fresh blueberry and raspberry flavors deliver a tart, refreshing ending to a meal. You will need silicone sphere molds but they are readily available online at a reasonable cost and really do help to make this dessert special.

Makes one 13½ x 4-inch (34.5 x 10-cm) tart

1 disc Sweet Tart Dough (page 24)

4 tbsp (60 ml) cold water, divided

1½ tsp (4.5 g) powdered, unflavored gelatin, divided

3 tbsp (42 g) butter, divided, diced

3 large eggs, divided

¾ cup (150 g) granulated sugar, divided

12 oz (340 g) fresh or frozen blueberries (thaw completely if using frozen), plus ¼ cup (37 g) fresh blueberries for decorating

¼ cup + 2 tbsp (90 ml) lemon juice

6 oz (170 g) fresh or frozen raspberries (thaw completely if using frozen), plus ¼ cup (30 g) fresh raspberries for decorating

Edible flowers, optional

Nonpareils

Equipment

4 x 13½–inch (10 x 34.5–cm) tart tin, approximately 1 inch (3 cm) deep

1½-inch (4-cm) sphere silicone mold (tray of at least six cavities)

1-inch (3-cm) sphere silicone mold (tray of at least twelve cavities)

Blueberry and Raspberry Curd Spheres Tart (Continued)

Make the Raspberry Curd

Place 2 tablespoons (30 ml) of the cold water in a medium bowl. Sprinkle ½ teaspoon of the gelatin over the water. Once the gelatin has bloomed, about 5 minutes, place 1 tablespoon (14 g) of the butter on top of the gelatin. Set a sieve over the bowl and set aside.

In a medium saucepan, whisk one egg with ¼ cup (50 g) of the sugar until thoroughly combined. Add 6 ounces (170 g) of the fresh or frozen raspberries (including juices if using frozen raspberries) and 2 tablespoons (30 ml) of the lemon juice. Heat the mixture on a medium-low setting, stirring constantly, until the raspberries have broken down and one or two bubbles burst through the surface of the curd (about 10 minutes) and the curd thickens (it should coat the back of a spoon). Immediately remove the saucepan from the heat and pour the mixture through the sieve and over the gelatin. Press on the solids to get as much raspberry mixture through as possible. Remove the sieve and discard the solids.

Whisk the raspberry–gelatin–butter mixture for 1 minute to ensure all the gelatin is dissolved.

Pour the curd into three of the remaining 1½-inch (4-cm) sphere cavities and six of the remaining 1-inch (3-cm) sphere cavities and level the top with an offset spatula. Place the two sphere mold trays in the freezer for 2 hours to firm up.

Assemble the Tart

Remove the tart from the refrigerator. Release the shell from the tart tin and place on a serving plate. Remove the two trays of sphere molds from the freezer. Push up gently from the bottom of the silicone mold to release each sphere. Slide a small, offset spatula under each raspberry and blueberry sphere and place it on the tart, using the photo as a reference for placement. Decoratively place the fresh blueberries and raspberries between the spheres. Sprinkle with some nonpareils and/or edible flowers if desired, and serve.

To Make Ahead or Store

The curd spheres can be made and frozen up to 3 days before they are to be eaten. The tart shell can be made up to 1 day ahead and stored, at room temperature, in an airtight container.

Assemble the tart on the day the tart is to be eaten.

Retro Baked Alaska Tartlets

Featured Decoration: Meringue Piping

Make the Gelato Domes
In each half-dome cavity, place four 1-tablespoon heaping scoops of the raspberry and pistachio gelato (for a total of eight scoops per mold). If the gelato is hard to scoop, let it warm on the counter for a few minutes. When the half-dome cavity is filled, use an offset spatula to push down on the gelato to remove any air pockets and smooth the top (photo A). Repeat the process for the other five half-dome cavities. Place the filled gelato molds in the freezer for at least 3 hours.

Make the Tartlet Shells
While the ice cream half-domes are chilling, adjust the oven rack to the lower-middle position and preheat the oven to 375°F (190°C). Combine the chocolate cookie crumbs and melted butter in a medium bowl. Divide the mixture among the six tartlet shells and press the mixture firmly into the sides and bottom of each shell. Place the tartlet shells on a baking sheet and transfer them to the oven. Bake for 7 minutes. Allow the shells to cool to room temperature, about 10 minutes, then place them in the freezer, on a parchment-lined baking sheet, to chill for at least 30 minutes before proceeding.

Assemble the Baked Alaska Tartlets
Remove the tartlet shells from the freezer and release them from their bases. Place 1 scant tablespoon (20 g) of raspberry jam into each shell. Remove the gelato half-domes from the freezer. Gently pop the half-domes from their molds and, using an offset spatula, place one half-dome in each of the prepared tart shells, flat side down (photo B). Return the filled tarts to the freezer on a parchment-lined baking sheet while you make the meringue.

(Continued)

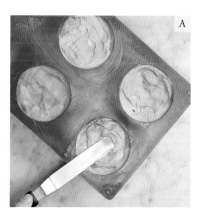

These cute Baked Alaska tartlets are a nod to the classic 1970s dessert in pie form, this time with a swirly, marshmallow-like exterior that hides mod gelato colors and a crunchy chocolate cookie crust inside. Express your inner 1970s style by choosing any ice cream or gelato color combination and decorating style that appeals to you.

Makes six 3-inch (8-cm) pies

1 cup (155 g) raspberry gelato

1 cup (155 g) pistachio gelato

1½ cups (120 g) chocolate cookie crumbs

¼ cup (60 g) unsalted butter, melted

6 tbsp (120 g) good-quality, seedless raspberry jam

3 large egg whites

⅛ tsp cream of tartar

Pinch of kosher salt

¾ cup (170 g) superfine sugar (see Note)

Equipment
1 six-cavity half-dome mold (2½-inch [6.5-cm] diameter for each cavity)

1 tablespoon-sized rounded scoop or melon scoop

Six 3-inch (8-cm) tart shells

Wilton 125 petal tip

Piping bag

Turntable

Kitchen torch

Retro Baked Alaska Tartlets (Continued)

Make the Meringue

Fill a large saucepan with 2 inches (5 cm) of water and bring to a simmer on the stovetop. Using a stand mixer fitted with a whisk attachment, whisk together the egg whites, cream of tartar, salt and sugar until combined. Set the bowl over the steaming water and, using a spatula, scrape down the sides and stir the mixture until the sugar has completely melted, about 5 minutes. To test this, pinch a small amount of the mixture between your fingers. If it feels grainy, continue to stir until the sugar has completely melted. Transfer the bowl back to the stand mixer and beat on high for 10 to 12 minutes, or until the meringue is thick and glossy, and is at room temperature (warm meringue will melt your gelato half-domes).

Decorate the Baked Alaska Tartlets

To decorate the tartlets, fit a piping bag with a Wilton 125 petal tip. Fill the piping bag with meringue. Remove one tartlet at a time from the freezer and place it on the turntable. Holding the piping bag in one hand, with the small end of the petal tip facing up, and pointed toward the center of the dome top, begin to apply even pressure to the piping bag as you turn the turntable slowly to pipe a circle of meringue around the top of the dome. Continue to pipe the meringue around the Alaska in a spiral, moving the turntable at a steady pace (photo C). Repeat for the remaining tartlets. Use a kitchen torch to lightly brown the tartlets (photo D). Place the tartlets back in the freezer until required.

Option:

For a simpler but still eye-catching decorating option, apply dollops of meringue to the tops of each tart (removing them from the freezer one at a time so they do not melt), and use a small offset spatula to swirl the meringue into a decorative pattern.

To Make Ahead or Store

The Baked Alaska Tartlets can be assembled up to 48 hours in advance, with the torched meringue topping, and stored in the freezer. To store the Baked Alaska Tartlets, insert toothpicks in the sides and top of each one before wrapping in plastic wrap. This will ensure that the wrap does not make direct contact with the meringue and mar the exterior.

Note:

You can make your own superfine sugar by processing granulated sugar in a food processor bowl for 2 to 3 minutes.

Roasted Vegetable Pithivier

Featured Decoration: Latticing

Prepare the Vegetables

Adjust the oven rack to the lower-middle position and preheat the oven to 400°F (205°C). Place the squash and red bell peppers on a baking sheet in a single layer and toss with 1 tablespoon (15 ml) of oil, ½ teaspoon of salt and ½ teaspoon of pepper.

Place the baking sheet in the oven and roast the vegetables for 25 minutes, or until softened, stirring once or twice. Remove the sheet from the oven. When cool enough to handle, remove the skin from the red bell pepper and slice into ½-inch (13-mm) pieces. Allow the vegetables to cool to room temperature. Lower the oven temperature to 350°F (175°C).

In the meantime, in a medium saucepan, melt the butter over medium heat. Add the mushrooms, onion, garlic, thyme, sage, ½ teaspoon of salt and ½ teaspoon of pepper and sauté until all the liquid has been absorbed, 8 to 10 minutes. Remove the saucepan from the heat, fold in the goat cheese and set aside.

In a medium skillet, sauté the asparagus in 1 teaspoon of the olive oil for 3 to 4 minutes, or until tender. Remove the skillet from the heat and allow the asparagus to cool to room temperature.

Prepare the Puff Pastry

Line a baking sheet with parchment paper and set aside. Lay one sheet of puff pastry on a lightly floured surface. Using an upside-down bowl with a 10-inch (25-cm) diameter, cut a 10-inch (25-cm) circle from the sheet. Gather the scraps and set aside. Lay out a second sheet of puff pastry. Using a bowl with a 12-inch (30-cm) diameter, cut a 12-inch (30-cm) circle. Place both circles on the baking sheet and transfer to the refrigerator to chill for 10 minutes.

(Continued)

A pithivier (pronounced "pee-tee-vee-YAY") is a round, domed puff pastry that originates from the French town of the same name. A classic pithivier is made with a sweet almond filling but I've loaded this version with roasted squash, peppers, onions, asparagus and creamy goat cheese. That said, feel free to substitute whatever vegetables you have on hand.

Makes one double-crust, 9-inch (23-cm) round pithivier

1 butternut squash, skinned, halved, deseeded and cut into 1-inch (3-cm) slices, approximately 3 cups (420 g)

2 red bell peppers, halved and deseeded

1 tbsp + 1 tsp (20 ml) olive oil, divided

1 tsp kosher salt, divided

1 tsp pepper, divided

1 tbsp (15 g) unsalted butter

½ lb (227 g) brown mushrooms, finely chopped (about 2 cups [150 g])

1 large onion, finely chopped (about 1 cup [150 g])

2 cloves garlic, minced

1 tsp thyme, chopped

1 tbsp (1 g) sage, chopped

2 oz (57 g) goat cheese, crumbled

1 bunch asparagus (12 to 16 stalks), trimmed

3 (12 x 15–inch [30 x 38–cm]) sheets pre-rolled frozen puff pastry, approximately ⅛ inch (3 mm) thick, thawed

1 large egg

1 tsp milk

Roasted Vegetable Pithivier (Continued)

Assemble the Pithivier

In a small bowl, whisk together the egg and milk to make the egg wash. Set aside.

Remove the puff pastry circles from the refrigerator. Working on the parchment-lined baking sheet, egg wash the 10-inch (25-cm) circle. Arrange the cooled roasted butternut squash in a fan pattern on the circle, leaving a 1-inch (3-cm) outer border. Next, evenly spread a layer of red bell pepper. Spoon the mushroom–onion–goat cheese mixture on top of the squash and red bell peppers. Lay the asparagus spears across the top of the goat cheese mixture. Using your hands, form the vegetables into a dome shape. Brush the border of the dough circle with egg wash. Lay the 12-inch (30-cm) circle of puff pastry over the mixture and press down all around the edges to completely seal the border. If the pastry circle is still too chilled and will not mold around the mixture, leave it to warm for a few minutes and then try again.

Lay out a third sheet of puff pastry. Roll a lattice roller (see the Sources section on page 180) along the pastry (photo A), then use your fingers to separate the lattice. Egg wash the entire top of the pithivier. Gently, transfer the lattice to the top of the pastry and drape it over the pithivier. Use your hands to smooth it in place, being sure to cover the entire dome (see Note). Using a small paring knife, cut away the overhang so you have a smooth circle shape again. You can also use the upside-down 12-inch (30-cm) bowl as a guide (photo B).

Egg wash the pithivier once again. Take the flat side of a knife and create vertical indentations all around the edge of the pie, at ½-inch (13-mm) intervals (photo C). Place the finished pithivier in the freezer for 10 minutes to firm up.

Bake the Pithivier

Remove the pithivier from the freezer. Place it, on the parchment-lined baking sheet, into the oven and bake for 45 to 50 minutes, or until golden brown. Allow it to cool slightly before serving.

To Make Ahead or Store

The vegetables can be prepared a day ahead and stored, tightly covered, in the refrigerator. The pithivier tastes best the day it is baked. Leftovers can be stored, in the refrigerator, for up to 2 days.

> **Note:**
> For a simpler decoration, use a sharp paring knife to trace a pattern of your choice on the top of the pithivier, being careful not to cut all the way through to the filling. The design will become more pronounced in the oven as the pithivier browns and puffs.

Equipment
Dough lattice cutter

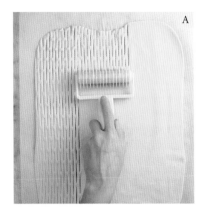

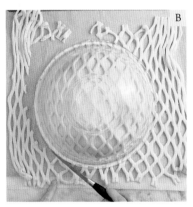

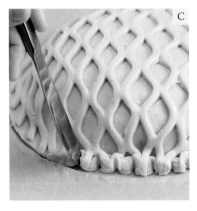

Tumbling Diamonds Blueberry-Lemon Pie

Featured Decoration: Diamond 3-D Pattern

Make the Pie Top

Remove one disc of the Everyday All-Butter Pie Dough from the refrigerator. On a lightly floured piece of parchment paper, roll out the dough to a 12-inch (30-cm) circle, approximately ⅛ inch (3 mm) thick. Turn the tart tin upside down on the dough. Score the outline of the tin lightly with a sharp knife (do not cut through the dough) then cut a circle that is 1 inch (3 cm) wider than the diameter (giving you a 10-inch [25-cm] circle). Slide the parchment, with the circle on it, onto a baking sheet and place it in the refrigerator. Keep the leftover scraps nearby.

Create the Diamond Decorations

Line a baking sheet with parchment paper. Remove the second disc of Everyday All-Butter Pie Dough from the refrigerator. Add the scraps from the first disc to it, then roll it out to a 12-inch (30-cm) circle, about ⅛ inch (3 mm) thick. With the 1-inch (3-cm) diamond-shaped cutter, cut 80 diamonds. Transfer them to the baking sheet and set aside. Set the leftover dough scraps aside.

Remove the disc of Chocolate Pie Dough from the refrigerator and roll it out to a 12-inch (30-cm) circle, about ⅛ inch (3 mm) thick. With the 1-inch (3-cm) diamond-shaped cutter, cut 80 diamonds. Add these to the parchment-lined sheet. Return the leftover dough scraps to the refrigerator for another use.

Remove the disc of Deep Purple Blueberry Pie Dough from the refrigerator. Roll out the dough to a 12-inch (30-cm) circle, about ⅛ inch (3 mm) thick. With the 1-inch (3-cm) diamond-shaped cutter, cut 80 diamonds. Transfer them to the baking sheet and set aside. Return the leftover dough scraps to the refrigerator for another use.

Decorate the Pie Top

In a small bowl, whisk together the egg and milk to make the egg wash. Set aside.

Remove the pie top from the refrigerator. Brush the pie top with egg wash. With a ruler, find the center of the circle and make a small mark. Place your first diamond on this spot. With the ruler as your guide, begin to place the other diamonds, alternating between all-butter, chocolate and blueberry diamonds, from the center to the top of the circle and then from the center to the bottom of the circle (photo A [page 99]). Extend the diamonds slightly over the border, both top and bottom (you will trim this later).

(Continued)

The tumbling diamond pattern may seem like it's having a moment now, but its origins go back to ancient Rome and Greece. Over the centuries, the block or diamond design has popped up time and time again in furniture, tile and wood designs. When you take the time to look at the clever optical illusion it creates, is it any wonder it continues to be so popular? This design involves a bit of diamond cutting (of the pastry kind) but it will be time well spent, I promise, when you mesmerize your friends and family with the finished effect.

Makes one 9-inch (23-cm) round pie

3 discs Everyday All-Butter Pie Dough (page 21)

1 disc Chocolate Pie Dough (page 21)

1 disc Deep Purple Blueberry Pie Dough (page 27)

1 large egg

1 tsp milk

¾ cup (150 g) granulated sugar

½ tsp kosher salt

⅓ cup (42 g) tapioca starch or cornstarch

5½ cups (814 g) blueberries

1 tbsp (15 ml) lemon juice

1 tsp lemon zest, finely grated

Equipment

9-inch (23-cm) tart tin with removable bottom

1-inch (3-cm) diamond-shaped cutter

Ruler

Tumbling Diamonds Blueberry-Lemon Pie (Continued)

For the second row, change the direction of the diamonds, continuing the color pattern that you established in the first row. Continue building rows, working out from the center, first on one side of the center row (photo B) and then the other until you have a completed design completely covering the pie top.

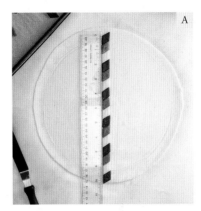

Turn the frame of the tart tin upside down and center it over the pie top. Using it as a cutter, press down to cut out the finished pie top (photo C). Place the pie top in the freezer to chill for 15 minutes.

Make the Pie Shell
Adjust the oven rack to the lower-middle position and place a baking sheet on it. Preheat the oven to 425°F (220°C). Remove the third disc of Everyday All-Butter Pie Dough from the refrigerator. Add the scraps from the second disc of Everyday All-Butter Pie Dough to the third disc. On a lightly floured surface, roll it out to a 12-inch (30-cm) circle. Transfer and fit the dough to the tart tin following the instructions in the Lining a Pie Plate or Tin section on pages 170 and 171, and trim the dough to the edge of the tart tin. Set the shell aside.

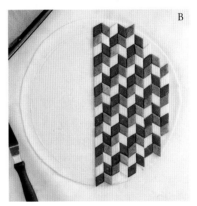

Make the Blueberry Filling
In a small bowl, whisk the sugar, salt and starch together. In a medium bowl, combine the blueberries, lemon juice and lemon zest. Sprinkle the sugar mixture over the blueberries and toss to thoroughly combine.

Assemble and Bake the Pie
Spoon the blueberry mixture into the pie shell. Brush the border of the pie with some egg wash. Remove the pie top from the freezer. Slide a pizza lifter or large spatula under the pie top and gently move it onto the prepared pie shell. Press lightly all around to ensure the top and the bottom are sealed together.

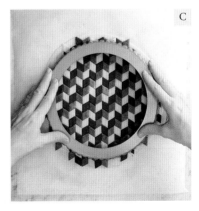

Make four thin vents in the top of the pie, between the diamonds. Transfer to the preheated baking sheet in the oven. Bake the pie for 15 minutes at 425°F (220°C), then turn the oven down to 375°F (190°C). Continue to bake for another 50 minutes, or until the top is golden brown. Allow the pie to cool for 3 hours before serving.

To Make Ahead or Store
The pie can be baked 1 day ahead and stored at room temperature, loosely covered. Leftover pie can be covered and stored at room temperature for up to 2 days.

The unbaked pie may be frozen, double wrapped, for up to 3 months. It must be baked from frozen. You may need to add an additional 10 to 15 minutes to the baking time for frozen pies.

Latticed Chicken Curry Pot Pie (page 109)

Chapter 5

Braid, Twist and Weave Patterns

Braids, twists and weaves are beautiful ways to add some glamour to your pie without a lot of practice or effort. As a bonus, the repetitive activity used to create these decorations can also be quite meditative and relaxing.

The decorative pies in this chapter use braids, twists and weaves in all sorts of creative ways. If you're looking to put a twist on the standard cobbler, try the Mixed Berry Cobbler with Lemon Buttermilk Twists (page 103). Practice your braiding skills with a two-tone multi-strand pie on the Sweet Cherry Pie with Two-Tone Braids (page 107). The Latticed Chicken Curry Pot Pie (page 109) will help you work on your pie dough embossing and latticing skills.

The step-by-step techniques for braiding, twisting and weaving pie dough can be found in Chapter 8: Essential Pie Skills and Decorating Techniques (page 167). Feel free to mix and match recipes with the designs in this chapter to create your own fabulous works of edible art.

Mixed Berry Cobbler with Lemon Buttermilk Twists

Featured Decoration: Pie Dough Twists

Make the Fruit Filling
Adjust the oven rack to the lower-middle position and preheat the oven to 375°F (190°C). Grease the baking pan with butter and set aside.

In a small bowl, whisk 1 cup (200 g) of the sugar with the tapioca or cornstarch and pinch of salt to combine. In a medium bowl, toss the blueberries, raspberries, blackberries, strawberries and lemon juice. Sprinkle the sugar-starch mixture over the berries and toss to combine. Set the bowl aside.

Make the Lemon Buttermilk Biscuit
Place 2 tablespoons (25 g) of the sugar in a medium bowl. Add the lemon zest, and using your fingertips, rub it into the sugar to release the essential oil from the lemon zest into the sugar. Add the flour, baking powder and ½ teaspoon of salt to the bowl. Whisk to combine. Add the butter to the bowl and toss well with a fork. Press the butter pieces between your fingers while working them into the sugar–flour mixture, until the butter resembles coarse meal (pea-sized pieces). Drizzle ½ cup (120 ml) of the buttermilk into the mixture while stirring with a fork. When the dough starts to form clumps, empty it onto a lightly floured counter and use your cupped hands to gather it together in a ball. Knead the dough a few times, just until it is smooth and comes together, being careful not to overknead.

Using a rolling pin, roll the dough out to a 6 x 10–inch (15 x 25–cm) rectangle. With a pizza cutter or knife and ruler, cut the dough lengthwise into twelve ½ x 10–inch (13-mm x 25-cm) strips. To make the twists, follow the directions in the Twist and Braiding Techniques section on pages 175 and 176. Repeat this process to make five more twists.

Assemble the Cobbler
Pour the fruit filling into the prepared pan and smooth the top. Place the six buttermilk biscuit twists across the width of the pan, spacing evenly. Trim the edges to fit the pan. Brush the biscuit twists with the remaining tablespoon (15 ml) of buttermilk and sprinkle with coarse sugar.

Bake the Cobbler
Bake the cobbler for 45 to 50 minutes, until the fruit bubbles thickly and the biscuit is golden brown. Cool the cobbler for 2 hours to ensure that the fruit filling is set.

To Make Ahead or Store
The cobbler is best eaten the day it is made. Leftovers can be covered and stored in the refrigerator for up to 2 days.

It's hard to beat a good fruit cobbler with its biscuit-like dough and bubbling fruit cooked in its own juices. This simple but tasty cobbler features a flaky, light lemon biscuit that gets a literal twist over a bevy of mixed berries. Serve with a little vanilla ice cream on the side for a casual but impressive dessert.

Makes one 9 x 13–inch (23 x 33–cm) cobbler

6 tbsp (85 g) unsalted butter, chilled, diced into ½-inch (13-mm) cubes, plus more for greasing

1 cup + 2 tbsp (225 g) granulated sugar, divided

⅓ cup (42 g) tapioca starch or cornstarch

½ tsp + a pinch of kosher salt, divided

2 cups (300 g) blueberries

1 cup (125 g) raspberries

1 cup (150 g) blackberries

1 cup (145 g) strawberries

1 tsp lemon juice

1 tsp lemon zest, finely grated

1½ cups (190 g) all-purpose flour

2 tsp (9 g) baking powder

½ cup + 1 tbsp (135 ml) buttermilk, chilled, divided

Coarse sugar, for sprinkling

Equipment
9 x 13–inch (23 x 33–cm) pan or dish with 2-inch (5-cm) sides

Pizza cutter

Ruler

Apricot and Blackberry Weave Galette

Featured Decorations: Apricot Weave, Freeform Pie Dough Border

Make the Blackberry Filling

In a small bowl, whisk together 1 cup (200 g) of the sugar, the tapioca or cornstarch and the salt. In a nonreactive, medium saucepan, combine the blackberries, water and lemon juice. Sprinkle the sugar-starch over the blackberry mixture. Set the heat to medium-low and stir the mixture with a heat-resistant spatula until the sugar has melted. Increase the temperature to medium and continue stirring until the mixture thickens, 7 to 10 minutes. Transfer the filling to a bowl and allow it to cool to room temperature, about 30 minutes.

Assemble the Galette

In a small bowl, whisk together the egg and milk to make the egg wash. Set aside.

Adjust the oven rack to the lower-middle position and preheat the oven to 375°F (190°C). On a piece of floured parchment paper, roll the disc of Everyday All-Butter Pie Dough to a 12-inch (30-cm) round. Spread the cooled blackberry filling over the base of the galette, leaving a 2-inch (5-cm) border all around. Sprinkle the amaretti crumbs evenly over the blackberry filling.

Cut the rounded edges off the top and bottom of each apricot half and set aside. Slice each trimmed apricot half into four even pieces (keeping each apricot together as a set). Arrange the apricots on the galette base in the following pattern: starting at the top left section of the circle, place four apricot slices vertically, then place four slices horizontally snuggly up against the vertical slices. Repeat this pattern, staying within the 2-inch (5-cm) border, until you have five rows across and down the galette. Sprinkle 2 tablespoons (25 g) of the granulated sugar evenly over the apricot slices.

Gently fold the pie dough edges up and over the outer ring of apricots. Brush the border with egg wash and sprinkle with slivered almonds.

Bake the Galette

Slide the galette, on the parchment sheet, onto a baking sheet. Place the galette in the oven and bake for 25 to 30 minutes, or until the pastry is browned and the blackberry filling begins to bubble. Remove the galette from the oven. In a small bowl, melt the apricot jam (if using) in the microwave for 15 seconds, then brush over the apricots. Let the galette rest for 30 minutes before serving.

To Make Ahead or Store

The galette is best eaten the day it is made. Leftovers can be covered and stored in the refrigerator for up to 2 days.

A simple galette involves nothing more than rolling some dough, plunking down some fruit and sugar in the middle, wrapping up the edges and tossing it in the oven. Easy peasy. In this version, I've amped things up a bit with a simple apricot weave and a sweet and jammy blackberry base to offset the tartness of the apricots. The amaretti cookie crumbs add a lovely almond flavor to the galette while helping to absorb some of the apricot juices.

Makes one 9-inch (23-cm) freeform galette

1 cup + 2 tbsp (225 g) granulated sugar, divided

¼ cup (32 g) tapioca flour or cornstarch

Pinch of kosher salt

2 cups (300 g) blackberries

1 tbsp (15 ml) water

2 tbsp (30 ml) lemon juice

1 large egg

1 tsp milk

1 disc Everyday All-Butter Pie Dough (page 21)

⅓ cup (30 g) amaretti cookies, crushed

11 apricots, halved lengthwise and pitted

1 cup (100 g) slivered almonds

2 tbsp (40 g) apricot jam, optional

Sweet Cherry Pie with Two-Tone Braids

Featured Decoration: Six-Strand Braids

Prepare the Pie Shell

Remove one disc of the Everyday All-Butter Pie Dough from the refrigerator. On a sheet of parchment paper, roll the dough out to a 12-inch (30-cm) circle, approximately ⅛ inch (3 mm) thick. Transfer and fit the dough into a 9-inch (23-cm) pie plate following the directions in the Lining a Pie Plate or Tin section on pages 170 and 171, and leaving a 1-inch (3-cm) overhang. Crimp the pie edges following the directions in the Crimping a Pie Edge section on page 179. Place the prepared pie shell in the refrigerator.

Make the Two-Tone Braids

Line a baking sheet with parchment paper. Remove the second disc of Everyday All-Butter Pie Dough from the refrigerator. On a lightly floured surface, roll the dough out to a 12-inch (30-cm) square, approximately ⅛ inch (3 mm) thick. Using a lattice cutter or a sharp knife and ruler, cut twenty-one ¼ x 10–inch (6-mm x 25-cm) strips of dough. Place on the baking sheet and set aside. Return the dough scraps to the refrigerator for another use.

Remove the disc of Chocolate Pie Dough from the refrigerator. On a lightly floured surface, roll the dough out to a 12-inch (30-cm) square, approximately ⅛ inch (3 mm) thick. Using a lattice cutter or a sharp knife and ruler, cut twenty-one ¼ x 10–inch (6-mm x 25-cm) strips of dough. Add to the baking sheet and set aside. Return the dough scraps to the refrigerator for another use.

Following the Six-Strand Braid directions in the Twist and Braiding Techniques section on page 176, make seven braids. Transfer the braids to the baking sheet and place in the refrigerator for 10 minutes.

Make the Cherry Filling

In a small bowl, whisk together the sugar, tapioca or cornstarch and salt. In a large bowl, toss the pitted cherries and lemon juice. Sprinkle the sugar-starch mixture over the cherries and toss to combine. Set aside.

(Continued)

I've always found that there is something strangely relaxing about braiding. Perhaps it's the repetitive action or the accomplishment I feel watching a design come together. Whatever the reason, I encourage you to give it a try. Keep your strands cold but pliable for the task at hand. This two-tone braid comes together quickly and the chocolate and butter pie doughs work beautifully with the sweet cherry filling.

Makes one 9-inch (23-cm) round pie

2 discs Everyday All-Butter Pie Dough (page 21)

1 disc Chocolate Pie Dough (page 21)

1 cup (200 g) granulated sugar

⅓ cup (42 g) tapioca starch or cornstarch

¼ tsp kosher salt

5 cups (770 g) pitted sweet cherries, fresh or frozen (defrosted)

1 tbsp (15 ml) fresh lemon juice

1 large egg

1 tsp milk

Equipment

9-inch (23-cm) standard pie plate

Lattice cutter

Ruler

Sweet Cherry Pie with Two-Tone Braids (Continued)

Decorate the Pie

Adjust the oven rack to the lower-middle position and place a baking sheet on it. Preheat the oven to 425°F (220°C). Remove the pie shell and braids from the refrigerator. Spoon the cherry pie filling into the shell. Using an offset spatula, carefully transfer the braids, one at a time, to the top of the pie. When you are happy with the placement, use a sharp knife to trim each end so they fit neatly against the dough edge. Place the decorated pie in the freezer for 30 minutes.

Bake the Pie

In a small bowl, whisk together the egg and milk to make the egg wash.

Remove the decorated pie from the freezer and brush it with the egg wash. Place the pie on the preheated baking sheet in the oven. Bake for 15 minutes at 425°F (220°C). Lower the temperature to 375°F (190°C) and continue to bake for another 50 to 60 minutes, until the filling bubbles in the middle of the pie and the pie is golden brown. Remove the pie from the oven and let it rest for at least 3 hours before serving.

To Make Ahead or Store

The pie can be baked 1 day ahead and stored at room temperature, loosely covered. Leftover pie can be covered and stored at room temperature for up to 2 days.

The unbaked pie may be frozen, egg washed and double wrapped, for up to 3 months. Bake directly from frozen at the temperature designated in the recipe. You may need to add an additional 10 to 15 minutes to the baking time for frozen pies.

Latticed Chicken Curry Pot Pie

Featured Decoration: Embossed Lattice

Make the Filling

Season the chicken pieces with salt and pepper. Heat the olive oil in a medium saucepan over medium heat. Cook the chicken until lightly browned on all sides, 5 to 7 minutes. Remove it from the saucepan and set aside. Add the onion, garlic, ginger and apple to the saucepan and cook, stirring often, until soft, about 5 minutes. Sprinkle the flour over the mixture and stir to combine. Add the curry powder and stir for 1 minute, until fragrant. Add the tomatoes with juices and the yogurt and stir, scraping up any brown bits from the bottom of the saucepan. Add the potato and simmer for 5 minutes. Stir in the mango chutney and remove the saucepan from the heat. Allow the mixture to cool to room temperature.

Create the Lattice

Remove one disc of the Golden Yellow Turmeric Pie Dough from the refrigerator. On a floured piece of parchment paper, roll out the dough to a 10-inch (25-cm) square. Using a lattice cutter or a sharp knife and ruler, cut twenty-four ¼ x 10–inch (6-mm x 25-cm) strips of dough. Place them on the parchment sheet. Slide the parchment sheet with the dough strips to a baking sheet and transfer to the refrigerator. Gather the leftover dough scraps and set aside.

Remove the second disc of Golden Yellow Turmeric Pie Dough from the refrigerator. Add any leftover dough from the first disc to the bottom of the second disc. On a floured piece of parchment paper, roll out the dough to a 10-inch (25-cm) square. Using a flower lace (or similar) impression mat and a rolling pin, emboss the dough, following the technique in the Embossing Pie Dough section on page 174. Depending on the size of your impression mat, you may need to reposition the mat a few times. Cut eight 1 x 10–inch (3 x 25–cm) strips of dough. Slide the parchment sheet with the dough strips onto a second baking sheet and set aside.

Lattice the Pie

Remove the first sheet of dough strips from the refrigerator and allow them to warm up for 3 to 5 minutes until they are pliable. On a piece of parchment paper, draw an 8-inch (20-cm) circle using the cake pan as your guide. Flip the parchment over and lay it on a flat surface. Lightly flour the parchment. Lay the eight 1 x 10–inch (3 x 25–cm) embossed strips of dough evenly across the circle. Then, following the technique in the Latticing a Pie section on pages 177 and 178, and working with three of the ¼ x 10–inch (6-mm x 25-cm) unembossed strips at a time, lay the sets perpendicular to the embossed strips, spacing the sets evenly across the pie. When you have finished the design, gently slide the parchment with the lattice onto a baking sheet and place it in the freezer for at least 15 minutes.

I adore a good Indian curry. And I love pie. It just makes sense, then, that I should marry the two in this delicious, fragrant and flaky package. This pie comes together quickly but has a depth of flavor that tastes like it took much longer. The turmeric in the dough adds a visual punch and a mild flavor that works beautifully with the curry. The embossed design pays homage to India's beautiful floral designs. Feel free to simplify this lattice or forgo it altogether if you choose. A solid pastry top with some flower cutout designs would look fabulous as well.

Makes one double-crust, 8-inch (20-cm) round pie

1 lb (454 g) boneless chicken thighs cut into ¾-inch (2-cm) pieces

½ tsp kosher salt

¼ tsp pepper

1 tbsp (15 ml) olive oil

1 large onion, chopped

2 cloves garlic, finely chopped

2 tbsp (12 g) grated fresh ginger

1 Granny Smith apple, peeled, cored and chopped into ½-inch (13-mm) pieces

1 tbsp (8 g) all-purpose flour

1 tbsp (7 g) medium or hot curry powder

1 cup (240 g) canned whole tomatoes, with juice

¼ cup (55 g) full-fat plain yogurt

(Continued)

Latticed Chicken Curry Pot Pie (Continued)

Make the Pie Shell
In a small bowl, whisk together the egg and milk to make the egg wash. Set aside.

Remove the third Golden Yellow Turmeric Pie Dough disc from the refrigerator. On a floured surface, roll out the dough to a 12-inch (30-cm) round. Gently transfer the dough to the cake pan following the directions in the Lining a Pie Plate or Tin section on pages 170 and 171 and trimming the overhang to 1 inch (3 cm). Spoon the cooled chicken curry filling into the pie shell. Brush the edges of the shell with the egg wash.

Assemble the Pie
Remove the lattice top from the freezer. Slide a pizza lifter or large spatula under the lattice and gently move it onto the prepared pie shell. Center the design on the pie top. The lattice top will be quite stiff, making it easy to adjust. When you are happy with the alignment, trim the edges of the lattice to the edge of the pie. Roll the overhang from the bottom shell up and over the pan edge to form a border. Using your baby finger, indent the dough all the way around the pie. Place the finished pie in the freezer for 30 minutes.

Adjust the oven rack to the lower-middle position and place a baking sheet on it. Preheat the oven to 425°F (220°C).

Bake the Pie
Transfer the pie to the baking sheet in the oven for 15 minutes at 425°F (220°C). Lower the temperature to 375°F (190°C) and bake for another 40 minutes until the pastry is golden and the filling is starting to bubble through the lattice. Remove the pie from the oven and allow it to cool for at least 15 minutes before serving.

To Make Ahead or Store
The pot pie is best eaten the day it is made. Leftovers can be covered and stored in the refrigerator for up to 2 days.

See baked photo on page 100.

1 russet potato, cut into ½-inch (13-mm) pieces

2 tbsp (40 g) mango chutney

3 discs Golden Yellow Turmeric Pie Dough (page 27)

1 large egg

1 tsp milk

Equipment
Lattice cutter

Ruler

Flower lace impression mat

8-inch (20-cm) round cake pan

Crisscross Cherry and Almond Braid

Featured Decoration: Braid

Make the Almond Filling
Using a stand or hand mixer, beat one egg, the butter and the almond extract on medium-high speed until creamy. Add ¼ cup (30 g) of confectioners' sugar, the almond meal and salt. Continue to beat, at a low speed, until just blended. Set aside.

Make the Cherry Filling
In a medium saucepan, combine the cherries, sugar, cornstarch and lemon juice. Using a potato masher or a fork, mash some of the cherries. Stir, over medium-low heat, until the cherries have softened and the mixture has thickened (about 5 minutes). Allow the mixture to cool to room temperature.

Make the Braid
In a small bowl, whisk together the second egg and 1 tablespoon (15 ml) of the milk to make the egg wash. Set aside.

Adjust the oven rack to the lower-middle position and preheat the oven to 375°F (190°C). On a lightly floured piece of parchment paper, roll out the sheet of puff pastry to a 12 x 14–inch (30 x 36–cm) rectangle. Using a sharp knife, cut away a 4 x 4–inch (10 x 10–cm) square from each of the four corners of the dough sheet. Cut slits down each side of the dough about 1 inch (3 cm) apart and 4 inches (10 cm) deep, leaving the center third of the dough uncut (photo A).

(Continued)

A

This impressive braid features a cherry–almond filling wrapped up in buttery puff pastry and baked to a golden brown. Best of all, it is quick and easy to make. Slice it into pieces or just let the crowd descend on it and pull it apart.

Makes one 10-inch (25-cm) braid

2 large eggs, divided

¼ cup (60 g) unsalted butter, room temperature, diced

1 tsp almond extract

¾ cup (90 g) confectioners' sugar, divided

½ cup (50 g) almond meal

Pinch of kosher salt

2 cups (310 g) cherries, halved and pitted, fresh or frozen (defrosted)

1 tbsp (13 g) sugar

1 tbsp (8 g) cornstarch

1 tsp lemon juice

2 tbsp (30 ml) milk, divided

1 (9-oz [255-g]) sheet frozen puff pastry, 12 x 14 inches (30 x 36 cm), thawed and chilled

1 tbsp (15 ml) cherry juice (from the defrosted cherries) or 1 drop pink food coloring

Equipment
Ruler

Crisscross Cherry and Almond Braid (Continued)

Spread the almond filling down the middle third of the dough sheet. Spoon the cooled cherry mixture on top of the almond filling. Fold the top and bottom rectangles of dough over the filling. Starting on the left-hand side, fold the first strip of dough across the center, wrapping it around to the other side on a diagonal. Take the first strip of dough from the right side and fold it over on a diagonal to the left side, slightly overlapping the left strip.

Continue folding strips of dough, crisscrossing the filling as you alternate strips from each side (photo B). When you reach the bottom, cut away any extra strips that you do not need (photo C). Tuck the end of the braid under and brush the entire surface with egg wash. Slide the braid, on the parchment paper, onto a baking sheet.

Bake the Braid
Place the braid in the oven and bake for 30 to 35 minutes, or until golden brown. Allow the braid to cool.

Make the Glaze
To make the cherry glaze, in a small bowl, combine ¼ cup (30 g) of the confectioners' sugar with the cherry juice (or 1 tablespoon [15 ml] of water mixed with 1 drop of pink food coloring). Mix until smooth.

To make the plain glaze, in a small bowl, combine ¼ cup (30 g) of the confectioners' sugar with 1 tablespoon (15 ml) of the milk. Mix until smooth.

Decorate the Braid
Drizzle the glazes across the cooled braid in a crisscross design.

To Make Ahead or Store
The braid can be baked 1 day ahead and stored at room temperature, loosely covered. Leftover braid can be covered and stored at room temperature for up to 2 days. The unbaked braid may be frozen, egg washed and double wrapped, for up to 3 months. It must be baked from frozen. You may need to add an additional 10 to 15 minutes to the baking time.

Rattan Chocolate Pecan Tart

Featured Decoration: Pecan Rattan

Make the Shell

Remove the disc of Everyday All-Butter Pie Dough from the refrigerator. On a lightly floured surface, roll out the disc to an 11-inch (28-cm) square, about ⅛ inch (3 mm) thick. Line the tart tin with the dough, following the technique in the Lining a Pie Plate or Tin section on pages 170 and 171. Trim the edge of the dough back to the edge of the tart tin. Return the shell to the refrigerator while you prepare the filling.

Make the Filling

Adjust the oven rack to the lower-middle position and place a baking sheet on it. Preheat the oven to 350°F (175°C). Measure out 1 cup (100 g) of pecans and set aside. In a medium skillet, toast the remaining ½ cup (50 g) of pecans over medium heat, watching carefully to ensure they do not burn. Set aside to cool.

To a medium bowl, add the melted butter and brown sugar and whisk the mixture until it is smooth. Add the flour, vanilla extract, corn syrup, eggs and bourbon (if using). Whisk to combine the ingredients. Coarsely chop the ½ cup (50 g) of the cooled toasted pecans and add them to the mixture. Stir in the chocolate pieces to combine. Remove the tart shell from the refrigerator and pour the mixture into it.

Decorate the Tart

To create the rattan design, start by placing one pecan vertically on top of the filling in the top left-hand corner of the tart. Place two more pecans horizontally next to the vertical pecans (photo A). Continue this pattern, left to right, from top to bottom to create a rattan (or weave) design (photo B).

(Continued)

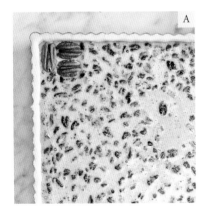

Anyone remember the 1970s when disco was in, dinner parties were all the rage and rattan furniture was everywhere? Decades later, rattan is back, this time as a design element on this deliciously melty chocolate pecan tart. This tart comes together quickly, and arranging those pecans in a rattan design will have you humming "Dancing Queen" in no time.

Makes one single-crust, 9-inch (23-cm) square tart

1 disc Everyday All-Butter Pie Dough (page 21), chilled

1½ cups (150 g) pecan halves, divided

2 tbsp (30 g) unsalted butter, melted

¾ cup (165 g) dark brown sugar

2 tbsp (15 g) flour

1 tsp pure vanilla extract

¾ cup (180 ml) dark corn syrup

3 large eggs, lightly beaten

2 tbsp (30 ml) bourbon, optional

¾ cup (150 g) good-quality semi-sweet chocolate, finely chopped

Equipment

9 x 9–inch (23 x 23–cm) tart tin with removable bottom, about 1 inch (3 cm) deep *or* a 9-inch (23-cm) standard round pie plate, about 1 inch (3 cm) deep (see Note)

Rattan Chocolate Pecan Tart (Continued)

Bake the Tart

Transfer the tart to the preheated sheet in the oven and bake for 50 to 55 minutes, or until the filling has puffed and the center is set. Let the tart cool for at least 1 hour before serving.

To Make Ahead or Store

The tart can be baked 1 day ahead and stored at room temperature, loosely covered. Rewarm it in a 325°F (165°C) oven for 10 to 15 minutes before serving. Leftover tart can be covered and stored in the refrigerator for up to 3 days.

This tart may be frozen, double wrapped, for up to 3 months. Allow it to defrost in the refrigerator overnight and then rewarm in the oven at 325°F (165°C) for 15 to 20 minutes.

Note:

This tart can be made in a standard, 9-inch (23-cm) round pie dish, although you will need to use a paring knife to cut the pecans on an angle so they fit snugly against the edge of the pan.

Christmas Gift Apple-Blackberry Pie (page 129)

chapter 6

Celebration Pies

Special occasion pies are some of my favorite pies to make because they remind me of the importance of family, friends and the value of traditions. The pies in this chapter will take you through a full year of celebrations, from birthday parties (Birthday Chocolate Banana Cream Pie, page 121) and Thanksgiving celebrations (Thanksgiving Turkey Pumpkin Pie, page 123) to a beautifully wrapped pie present (Christmas Gift Apple-Blackberry Pie, page 129) and an impressive way to ring in the new year (New Year's Raspberry Champagne Tart, page 135). These pies can be made with as many or as few decorations as it takes to make your occasion special and full of memories.

Birthday Chocolate Banana Cream Pie

Featured Decoration: Piping

Make the Cookie Crust
Adjust the oven rack to the lower-middle position and preheat the oven to 350°F (175°C).

In a medium bowl, mix the digestive cookie crumbs and the butter until thoroughly combined. Press the mixture evenly across the bottom and about 2 inches (5 cm) up the sides of the springform pan. Transfer the pan to the oven and bake the cookie crust for 10 minutes. Allow it to cool to room temperature before proceeding.

Make the Chocolate Pastry Cream
Place a sieve over a medium bowl and set aside. In another medium bowl, whisk together the egg yolks, tapioca flour or cornstarch, sugar and vanilla until smooth. Set aside. In a medium saucepan over medium heat, bring the milk and heavy cream to a simmer. Remove from the heat.

In a slow, steady stream, whisk half of the warm milk/cream mixture into the egg mixture. Do not add all the warm milk mixture at once or you will curdle the eggs. Slowly stream the combined mixture back into the saucepan containing the remainder of the milk/cream and heat over a medium-low heat, stirring constantly with a wooden spoon, until the custard begins to thicken and a few bubbles burst through on the surface. Immediately pour the custard through the sieve set over the bowl. Remove the sieve and add the butter and the chopped chocolate. Whisk until completely melted.

Place plastic wrap directly on top of the chocolate pastry cream, to prevent a skin from forming. Chill for at least 30 minutes in the refrigerator.

Assemble the Pie
Slice the four bananas into ¼-inch (6-mm) slices and place them in a bowl. Add the lemon juice and toss until the bananas are well coated (this will keep the bananas from browning). Place half of the bananas in a single layer at the bottom of the cooled cookie shell. Spoon half the chocolate pastry cream over the bananas and smooth with an offset spatula. Add the remainder of the bananas in a single layer, followed by the remaining chocolate pastry cream. Smooth the top with an offset spatula. Place the pie in the refrigerator to chill for at least 2 hours.

(Continued)

With luscious chocolate pastry cream, bananas and a super buttery cookie crust, this pie brings up all sorts of wonderful memories of the cream pies my mom used to make. While you can keep it simple, I think the festive decorating style would make this the perfect gift for the banana-loving birthday boy or girl in your life. The digestive cookie base gives the pie a nice crunch and complements the creamy chocolate banana filling perfectly.

Makes one 8-inch (20-cm) round pie

Cookie Crust
8 oz (227 g) digestive cookies, crushed

½ cup (120 g) unsalted butter, melted

Chocolate Pastry Cream
3 large egg yolks

5 tbsp (40 g) tapioca flour or cornstarch

¾ cup (150 g) granulated sugar

1½ tsp (8 ml) pure vanilla extract

2½ cups (600 ml) whole milk

½ cup (120 ml) heavy cream

2 tbsp (30 g) unsalted butter, diced

3 oz (85 g) semisweet chocolate, finely chopped

Banana Layer
4 bananas, ripe but still firm

1 tbsp (15 ml) lemon juice

Birthday Chocolate Banana Cream Pie (Continued)

Place the heavy cream, sugar and vanilla in a medium bowl. Using a stand mixer with a whisk attachment or a hand mixer, beat the heavy cream to stiff peaks. Place the heavy cream in a piping bag fitted with a Wilton 1M tip. Holding the piping bag over the pie, apply even pressure to pipe decorative "squiggles" all over the top of the pie.

Just before serving, slice the final banana into ½-inch (13-mm) slices and place decoratively between the piped whipped cream. Add the maraschino cherries (if using). Sprinkle the top of the pie with nonpareils and then drizzle with chocolate sauce. Serve immediately.

To Make Ahead or Store
The cookie crust and chocolate pastry cream can be made, separately, 1 day ahead. Keep the cookie crust wrapped and on the counter. The chocolate pastry cream should be stored in a container, covered in plastic wrap, in the refrigerator. The pie is best assembled on the day it is to be served. Leftovers can be stored in the refrigerator, tightly wrapped, for up to 2 days.

Decorations

1 cup (240 ml) heavy cream

1 tbsp (12 g) granulated sugar

1 tsp pure vanilla extract

1 banana, ripe but still firm

6 to 8 whole maraschino cherries with stems, optional

2 tbsp (24 g) multicolored nonpareils

¼ cup (60 ml) good-quality chocolate sauce

Equipment

8-inch (20-cm) springform pan with a removable bottom, about 3 inches (8 cm) deep

Piping bag

Wilton 1M tip

Thanksgiving Turkey Pumpkin Pie

Featured Decorations: Stencil Cutouts, Pie Dough Leaves, Mottled Pie Dough

Prepare the Stencil and Pie Top

To make the stencil, copy the pattern on page 127 on a piece of 8½ x 11–inch (22 x 28–cm) paper. Cut out the turkey body and feather border and set aside.

Remove one disc of the Everyday All-Butter Pie Dough from the refrigerator. On a lightly floured piece of parchment paper, roll out the dough to a 12-inch (30-cm) round, approximately ⅛ inch (3 mm) thick. Turn the pie pan upside down and use a sharp knife to cut out a 9-inch (23-cm) circle of dough. Slide the parchment, with the dough circle on it, onto a baking sheet and transfer it to the refrigerator to chill for 10 minutes. Gather up the remaining scraps of dough and set aside.

Prepare the Pie Shell

Remove the second disc of the Everyday All-Butter Pie Dough from the refrigerator. On a lightly floured surface, roll out the dough to a 12-inch (30-cm) circle, approximately ⅛ inch (3 mm) thick. Transfer and fit the dough to the pie plate, following the directions in the Lining a Pie Plate or Tin section on pages 170 and 171, leaving a 1-inch (3-cm) overhang. Fold the overhang under the pie plate rim and use the baby finger on your dominant hand, angled, to create impressions around the edge of the pie (or create any border that you wish). Add the leftover dough scraps to those from the pie top and set aside. Place the pie shell in the refrigerator to chill for 15 minutes.

(Continued)

If you're looking for a show-stopping Thanksgiving pie, you've come to the right page. This pie's custardy filling is pure nostalgia with just the right balance of spices and pumpkin flavor, and it pairs perfectly with the flaky all-butter pastry. The filling comes together quickly so you have more time to work on your decorations. The top is baked separately and then assembled on the pie after baking.

Makes one 9-inch (23-cm) round pie

2 discs Everyday All-Butter Pie Dough (page 21)

1 disc Chocolate Pie Dough (page 21)

4 large eggs, divided

1 tsp milk

2 cups (480 g) pumpkin puree

1 cup (240 ml) heavy cream

1 cup (220 g) dark brown sugar

1 tsp ground cinnamon

½ tsp ground ginger

½ tsp kosher salt

¼ tsp ground nutmeg

⅛ tsp ground cloves

Equipment

Turkey Body and Feather Border Stencil (see page 127)

Standard 9-inch (23-cm) pie plate

1½-inch (4-cm) leaf cutter

1-inch (3-cm) leaf cutter

2-inch (5-cm) assorted leaf cutters (maple leaf, oak leaf, etc.)

½-inch (13-mm) circle cutter or plain round pastry tip

Thanksgiving Turkey Pumpkin Pie (Continued)

Cut the Stencil and Make the Decorations

Remove the pie top from the refrigerator. Position the turkey body stencil 1¾ inches (4 cm) in from the right edge of your pie top and centered, top to bottom. Use a sharp knife or precision knife to cut out the turkey body (photo A). Position the feather border stencil 3¾ inches (10 cm) from the left side of the pie top and centered, top to bottom, and cut the tail border. Return the dough circle to the refrigerator.

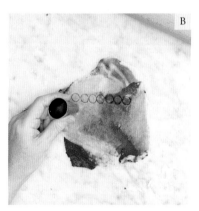

Add the dough scraps from the stencil cutouts to the leftover scraps from the pie top and shell and roll them out to a circle, approximately ⅛ inch (3 mm) thick. Using a 1½-inch (4-cm) leaf cutter, cut twenty leaves (for the feathers). Using a 1-inch (3-cm) leaf cutter, cut twenty-four leaves (for the border), rerolling the dough if necessary. Place all the leaves on the baking sheet. Set the leftover scraps aside.

Remove the disc of Chocolate Pie Dough from the refrigerator. On a lightly floured surface, roll out the dough to a 12-inch (30-cm) circle, approximately ⅛ inch (3 mm) thick. Using 2-inch (5-cm) leaf cutters of your choice, cut out twelve chocolate leaves (for the feathers). Using a 1-inch (3-cm) leaf cutter, cut twenty-four leaves (for the border). Cut small pieces of dough to represent the turkey's beak, wattle and feet. Place the leaves and decorations on the baking sheet.

To create the mottled pie dough for the short feathers, gather the leftover all-butter and chocolate dough scraps together in a ball. On a lightly floured surface, roll the dough out to a circle, approximately ⅛ inch (3 mm) thick. Using a decorating tip or cutter with a ½-inch (13-mm) opening, cut 24 mottled circles (photo B). Add these to the baking sheet with the other decorations. Transfer the baking sheet to the refrigerator to chill.

(Continued)

Thanksgiving Turkey Pumpkin Pie (Continued)

Assemble the Pie Top

Adjust the oven rack to the lower-middle position and preheat the oven to 375°F (190°C).

In a small bowl, whisk together one of the eggs and the milk to make the egg wash. Set aside.

Remove the two baking sheets containing the pie top and decorations from the refrigerator. Brush the surface of the pie top with egg wash. On the left side of the feather border cutout, about ½ inch (13 mm) from the edge of the cutout, place the twelve chocolate 2-inch (5-cm) leaves, in a fan shape, slightly overlapping them as you go. Place the all-butter dough 1½-inch (4-cm) leaves in a fan shape against the edge of the feather border cutout, overlapping the chocolate leaf feathers slightly (photo C).

On the right side of the feather border cutout, pile the marbleized circles randomly to resemble ruffled feathers (photo D). Brush more egg wash around the border of the pie top. Alternate the 1-inch (3-cm) chocolate leaves and the 1-inch (3-cm) all-butter dough leaves around the border of the pie (photo E). Add the small pieces of dough that represent the turkey's beak, wattle and feet.

Brush all the leaves and decorations with egg wash. Return the decorated pie top, on the baking sheet, to the freezer for 15 minutes to firm up.

Bake the Pie Top

Using a spatula, transfer the pie top to another parchment-lined baking sheet (the one that has been in the freezer is too cold for the oven). Place the pie top in the oven and bake for 20 to 25 minutes, until golden brown. Remove and allow the top to cool on the baking sheet while you make the filling. Leave the oven set to 375°F (190°C).

Make the Pumpkin Filling

Whisk the remaining three eggs in a large bowl until combined. Add the pumpkin puree, heavy cream, brown sugar, cinnamon, ginger, salt, nutmeg and cloves and stir to combine.

Bake the Pie

Pour the filling into the chilled pie shell. Place the pie on a rimmed baking sheet (this will make it easier to move the pie in and out of the oven) and transport it carefully to the center rack of the oven. Bake for 40 minutes. Remove the pie from the oven. Using a large spatula or a pizza lifter, slide the baked pie top onto the pie. Return the pie to the oven and bake for another 10 to 12 minutes, or until the filling is puffed but still slightly wobbly in the center. If you have a digital thermometer, place it in the center of the pie to check for a temperature of between 175°F (80°C) and 180°F (85°C). Allow the pie to cool for at least 3 hours before serving. The filling will continue to set as it cools.

To Make Ahead or Store

The pumpkin pie filling can be made 1 day in advance and stored, tightly covered, in the refrigerator. Leftovers can be stored in the refrigerator, covered loosely with plastic wrap, for up to 3 days.

Stencil Template

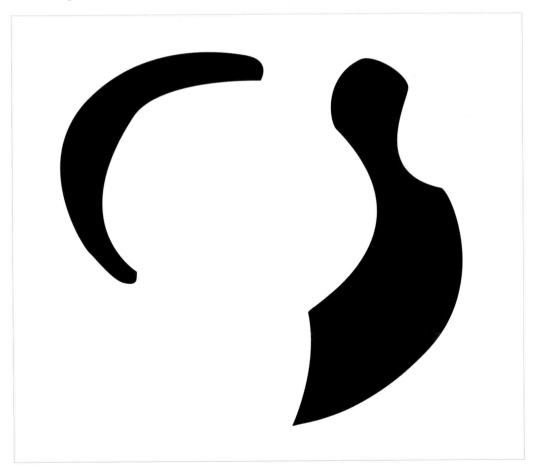

Christmas Gift Apple-Blackberry Pie

Featured Decorations: Pie Dough Braids, Branches, Ornaments & Leaves

Make the Pie Shell

Remove one disc of the Everyday All-Butter Pie Dough from the refrigerator. On a lightly floured surface, roll the dough into a 13-inch (33-cm) square. Fit the dough to the tart tin, following the directions in the Lining a Pie Plate or Tin section on pages 170 and 171, and leaving a 1-inch (3-cm) overhang. Place the shell in the refrigerator to chill while you prepare the filling. Add any scraps of dough to the bottom of the second disc of dough in the refrigerator.

Make the Filling

In a deep skillet or Dutch oven, melt the butter over medium heat. Add the apples, tapioca starch or cornstarch, sugar, cinnamon and lemon juice. Cook, stirring frequently, until the apples start to soften and the juices have thickened, 5 to 7 minutes. Add the blackberries and cook for another 2 minutes, stirring gently to avoid breaking up the blackberries. Remove the mixture from the heat and allow it to cool to room temperature before proceeding.

Make the Decorations

Line a baking sheet with parchment paper. Remove the second disc of Everyday All-Butter Pie Dough from the refrigerator. Cut off three walnut-sized pieces of dough from the disc and roll each into a ball approximately 1½ inches (4 cm) in diameter. While the dough is still cold, use a ½-inch (13-mm) cookie cutter of your choice to make impressions in various spots all around each of the three balls. Set the balls aside on the baking sheet.

To make the pine branches, cut a walnut-sized piece of dough from the disc and roll it out into a long, narrow tube. Lying it flat, use a sharp knife to make diagonal incisions down both sides of the tube. Repeat this process twice more to make three fir branches. Add the branches to the baking sheet with the balls.

On a lightly floured surface, roll out the remainder of the dough from the second disc to a 7 x 12–inch (18 x 30–cm) rectangle. Cut six ½ x 12–inch (13-mm x 30-cm) strips of dough. Roll the strips gently on a floured surface to give them rounded edges. Use the strips to make three twists following the Twist directions in the Twist and Braiding Techniques section on page 175. Set the twists on the baking sheet with the other decorations. Place the baking sheet in the refrigerator. With the remaining dough, cut sixteen 1-inch (3-cm) stars, twelve 2-inch (5-cm) stars, eight 3-inch (8-cm) stars and three 1-inch (3-cm) holly leaves, rerolling the dough if necessary. Place the stars on the baking sheet with the twists.

(Continued)

I love giving pies as gifts and I adore making pies that look like gifts. So, in the spirit of "it's better to give than receive," I present this beautifully wrapped Christmas pie. You can make the pie exactly as shown here but feel free to simplify the decorations by just making the bow, or by creating your own gift wrap design.

Makes one 10-inch (25-cm) square pie

3 discs Everyday All-Butter Pie Dough (page 21)

1 tbsp (15 g) unsalted butter

2 lb (907 g) apples (Gala, Spy, Cortland, Golden Delicious or a mix), peeled, cored and cut into ¼-inch (6-mm) slices

¼ cup (32 g) tapioca starch or cornstarch

½ cup (100 g) granulated sugar

1 tsp ground cinnamon

1 tbsp (15 ml) lemon juice

1½ cups (215 g) blackberries

1 large egg

1 tsp milk

Equipment

10-inch (25-cm) square tart tin, about 1 inch (3 cm) deep

½-inch (13-mm) cookie cutter of your choice

1-inch (3-cm) star cutter

2-inch (5-cm) star cutter

3-inch (8-cm) star cutter

1-inch (3-cm) holly cutter

Ruler

Christmas Gift Apple-Blackberry Pie (Continued)

Assemble the Pie

In a small bowl, whisk together the egg and milk to make the egg wash. Set aside.

Adjust the oven rack to the lower-middle position and place a baking sheet on it. Preheat the oven to 425°F (220°C). Remove the pie shell from the refrigerator. Spoon the cooled fruit filling into the shell, levelling the top with an offset spatula.

Roll out the third disc of Everyday All-Butter Pie Dough to a 12-inch (30-cm) square. Brush around the edges of the pie shell with the egg wash. Loosely wrap the rolled-out piece of dough around the rolling pin and gently unroll it onto the filling. Press gently all around the edge of the pie to ensure that the bottom pie dough adheres to the top. Trim the pie to just beyond the edge of the tart tin and wrap the pie dough around the edges. Press firmly so the dough adheres to the tin. Lightly brush the egg wash across the surface of the pie top. Place the pie dough stars on the pie top in a decorative pattern, wrapping a few around the edges of the pie. Center and cross two of the 12-inch (30-cm) twists in the middle of the pie. Wrap the edges of the twists around the edge of the pie and trim. Cut the third twist in half. Create two loops by pinching the ends of each twist together. Place the loops in the center of the pie where the braids meet. Add the fir branches to the center of the pie, so they point up to the top left-hand corner of the pie and cover the end of the twist loops. Place the three ornaments in the center of the pie. Finally, place the holly leaf cutouts around the ornaments. Cut vents in the pie between the fir leaves and under the twists. Brush the top of the pie with more egg wash. Transfer it to the freezer for 30 minutes.

Bake the Pie

Place the pie on the baking sheet in the oven. Bake the pie at 425°F (220°C) for 15 minutes. Reduce the heat to 375°F (190°C) and bake for another 50 to 60 minutes until the crust is golden. Allow the pie to cool for at least 3 hours before serving.

To Make Ahead or Store

The pie can be baked 1 day ahead and stored at room temperature, loosely covered. Leftover pie can be covered and stored at room temperature for up to 2 days.

The unbaked pie may be frozen, egg washed and double wrapped, for up to 3 months. It must be baked from frozen. You may need to add an additional 10 to 15 minutes to the baking time for frozen pies.

See baked photo on page 118.

Holiday Lights Mincemeat Tart

Featured Decorations: Pie Dough Twists & Lightbulbs

Make the Mincemeat

Place the apples, golden and dark raisins, currants, candied citrus peel, brown sugar, maple syrup, beef suet or butter, brandy, orange juice, zest, allspice and nutmeg in a medium-sized saucepan or Dutch oven over medium-low heat and cook for 20 to 25 minutes, stirring often, until the fruit has softened and the liquid has been absorbed. Allow the mixture to cool to room temperature.

Prepare the Tart Shell

Adjust the oven rack to the lower-middle position and place a baking sheet on it. Preheat the oven to 375°F (190°C). Remove one disc of Citrus-Scented Tart Dough from the refrigerator. On a lightly floured surface, roll out the dough to a 7 x 16–inch (18 x 41–cm) rectangle. Fit the dough to the tart tin following the directions in the Lining a Pie Plate or Tin section on pages 170 and 171, leaving a 1-inch (3-cm) overhang. Partially blind bake the shell following the directions in the Partial and Full Blind Baking section on pages 172 and 173. After baking, allow the shell to cool slightly, then trim the excess pie dough with a sharp knife.

Make the Decorations

In a small bowl, whisk together the egg and milk to make the egg wash. Set aside.

Line a baking sheet with a sheet of parchment paper. Remove the second disc of Citrus-Scented Tart Dough from the refrigerator. On a lightly floured surface, roll the dough out to an 8 x 12–inch (20 x 30–cm) rectangle. With a 1-inch (3-cm) lightbulb cookie cutter, cut out fourteen dough lightbulbs. Place the bulbs on the baking sheet. Brush the bulb section (not the stem) with some egg wash and sprinkle with silver or gold nonpareils (or a combination of both). Set aside to dry.

With a sharp knife and a ruler, cut ten ¼ x 8–inch (6-mm x 20-cm) strips of dough from the same rolled-out piece of dough. Roll each strip gently on the floured surface to round out the edges. Using two strips at a time, twist the dough, following the Twist directions in the Twist and Braiding Techniques section on page 175, to resemble the wire on a string of lights. When finished, you should have five sets of twisted dough strings. Set them aside on the baking sheet.

(Continued)

Mincemeat tarts are one of the quintessential British desserts during the holidays and with good reason. Don't be put off by the name (there is actually no meat in the recipe) or by the fact that the recipe calls for beef suet. You can easily substitute butter. The lightbulb strings in gold and silver tones give this tart a festive feel.

Makes one 4 x 13¹/₂-inch (10 x 34.5-cm) rectangular tart

2 apples (Gala, Spy, Cortland, Golden Delicious or a mix), peeled, cored and finely chopped

½ cup (80 g) golden raisins

½ cup (80 g) dark raisins

½ cup (80 g) dried currants

⅓ cup (25 g) candied citrus peel

⅓ cup (75 g) packed dark brown sugar

¼ cup (60 ml) maple syrup

⅓ cup (68 g) beef suet or 3 tbsp (45 g) unsalted butter

¼ cup (60 ml) brandy

2 tbsp (30 ml) orange juice

2 tsp (4 g) finely grated fresh orange zest

½ tsp ground allspice

¼ tsp ground nutmeg

2 discs Citrus-Scented Tart Dough (page 25)

1 large egg

1 tsp milk

Gold and silver nonpareils

Holiday Lights Mincemeat Tart (Continued)

Assemble and Bake the Tart

Fill the cooled tart shell with the cooled mincemeat mixture. Pick up one dough "string" and loop it in a back-and-forth motion down the tart. Add the other four strings to cover the entire length of the tart, joining the light strings by pinching them together (photo A).

Place the lightbulbs decoratively amongst the light strings, being sure to cover the places where they join together (photo B). Brush the pie edges and the strings with egg wash and place the tart in the oven. Bake for 25 to 30 minutes, or until the pastry is golden brown. Remove the tart from the oven and allow it to cool to room temperature, about 1 hour.

To Make Ahead or Store

The tart can be made 1 day ahead and then gently reheated for 15 to 20 minutes, covered loosely with tinfoil, at 300°F (150°C) before serving. Leftovers can be stored in the refrigerator, covered loosely with plastic wrap, for up to 3 days.

Note:

If you have trouble finding a lightbulb cutter, star cutouts would work beautifully here as well.

Equipment

4 x 13½–inch (10 x 34.5–cm) rectangular tart tin with removable bottom, about 1 inch (3 cm) deep

1-inch (3-cm) lightbulb cutter

Ruler

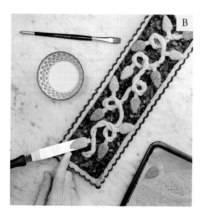

New Year's Raspberry-Champagne Tart

Featured Decorations: Pie Dough Stars, Sugared Grapes, Bubble Sugar

Prepare the Tart Shell

Adjust the oven rack to the lower-middle position and place a baking sheet on it. Preheat the oven to 425°F (220°C). Remove the disc of Chocolate Pie Dough from the refrigerator. On a lightly floured surface, roll the dough out to an 11 x 14–inch (28 x 36–cm) rectangle. Gently transfer and fit the dough to the tart tin, following the directions in the Lining a Pie Plate or Tin section on pages 170 and 171, and leaving a 1-inch (3-cm) overhang. Fully blind bake the tart shell, following the directions in the Partial and Full Blind Baking section on pages 172 and 173.

Gather the leftover dough scraps and return them to the refrigerator. After baking, allow the pie shell to cool slightly before using a sharp knife to cut away the excess dough around the edges.

Make the Champagne Panna Cotta

Place ¼ cup (60 ml) of the champagne or sparkling wine in a small bowl. Sprinkle the gelatin over it and leave it to soften for 5 minutes. In a medium saucepan, combine the remaining ¼ cup (60 ml) of champagne with the heavy cream, sugar, salt and vanilla. Warm the mixture over medium heat until the sugar dissolves and the mixture just starts to steam (do not allow it to boil). Remove the saucepan from the heat and whisk in the gelatin mixture. Pour the mixture into the cooled shell and refrigerate for at least 2 hours and up to 24 hours.

Make the Raspberry Gelée

Place a fine-mesh sieve over a small bowl and set aside. Pour ¼ cup (60 ml) of water into a small saucepan. Sprinkle the gelatin over the water. Add the raspberries, sugar and lemon juice and simmer, stirring constantly, until the raspberries break down and the sugar dissolves, about 5 minutes.

Pour the mixture through the sieve, pressing on the raspberries with a spatula or wooden spoon to get as much pulp and juice through as possible. Discard the strained seeds. Allow the gelée to cool for 10 minutes, then pour it over the cooled and set panna cotta. Return the tart to the refrigerator to cool and set, about 2 hours.

(Continued)

This decadent dessert is the perfect way to welcome the new year in style. I mean, c'mon, that color! The combination of chocolate, champagne, raspberries and sugar-frosted grapes (with a sprinkling of blingy stars) creates a luscious and creamy dessert that your guests won't soon forget. It is deceptively easy to make but, if you're feeling wrung out from the holidays, feel free to skip the decorations and go with a simple fruit border instead.

Makes one 8 x 11–inch (20 x 28–cm) tart

Tart Shell

1 disc Chocolate Pie Dough (page 21)

Champagne Panna Cotta

½ cup (120 ml) chilled champagne or sparkling wine, divided

2 tsp (6 g) unflavored, powdered gelatin

2 cups (480 ml) heavy cream

⅓ cup (67 g) granulated sugar

Pinch of kosher salt

1 tsp pure vanilla extract

Raspberry Gelee

1½ tsp (4.5 g) gelatin

1½ cups (185 g) raspberries

¼ cup (50 g) granulated sugar

1 tsp fresh lemon juice

New Year's Raspberry-Champagne Tart (Continued)

Make the Decorations

In a small bowl, whisk together the egg white and salt. Set aside.

Line a baking sheet with parchment paper. Adjust the oven rack to the lower-middle position and place a baking sheet on it. Preheat the oven to 350°F (175°C). Roll out the scraps of Chocolate Pie Dough to a ⅛-inch (3-mm) thickness. Cut out five 1-inch (3-cm) stars and five 1½-inch (4-cm) stars. Brush some egg mixture on each star and sprinkle with some of the gold pearlized sugar. Shake off the excess sugar and set aside. Place the stars on the baking sheet and bake for 10 minutes or until firm. Allow the stars to cool. Turn the oven temperature down to 300°F (150°C).

To make the sugared grapes, pour the granulated sugar in a shallow dish. Line a baking sheet with parchment paper. Place the grapes in the bowl of the leftover egg white, stir to coat and transfer with a fork to the dish of granulated sugar. Roll the grapes in the sugar to coat them, then move them to the baking sheet to dry.

To make the bubble sugar, lay a silicone baking mat on a baking sheet. Using an offset spatula, spread the glycerin in a thin layer over the mat. Sprinkle the remaining gold pearlized sugar over the glycerine. Place the mixture in the oven and bake at 300°F (150°C) for 30 minutes, or until it bubbles. Remove the sheet from the oven and allow the bubble sugar to cool for 5 minutes before breaking it into irregular-shaped pieces.

Decorate the Tart

To ensure that your decorations look their best, decorate the tart within a few hours of serving it. To decorate the tart, place the raspberries down the center of the tart, alternating them left and right of the center line. Place the sugared grapes down the center as well, in the opposite left/right position to the raspberries. Next, place groupings of stars decoratively down the tart, filling in any large gaps. Sprinkle the gold nonpareils down both sides of the center decoration. Place the sugar bubble pieces decoratively amongst the raspberries and grapes.

To Make Ahead or Store

The tart can be baked 1 day ahead and stored in the refrigerator, wrapped in tinfoil. Plastic wrap will cling to the surface and mar the finish. Leftover tart can be covered and stored at room temperature for up to 2 days.

Note:

Glycerin can be found at baking and craft stores and some grocery stores under the Wilton brand name. If you have trouble locating it, this decoration can be replaced with a few more pie dough cutouts (your choice of design) using leftover scraps of Chocolate Pie Dough. Bake them at 350°F (175°C) for about 10 minutes before adding them to the tart.

Decorations

1 large egg white

Pinch of salt

¼ cup (50 g) gold pearlized sugar

¼ cup (50 g) granulated sugar

12 purple grapes

¼ cup (80 g) glycerin (see Note)

10 raspberries

Gold nonpareils, optional

Equipment

8 x 11–inch (20 x 28–cm) tart tin with removable bottom, about 1 inch (3 cm) deep

1-inch (3-cm) star cutter

1½-inch (4-cm) star cutter

Silicone mat

Easter Basket Pizza Pie

Featured Decorations: Pie Dough Twists, Butterflies & Flowers

Make the Pie Shell

Line a baking sheet with parchment paper. Cut another piece of parchment 8 x 12 inches (20 x 30 cm) and place it inside the loaf pan with an equal amount of overhang on both sides of the pan. The parchment will serve as handles to help you remove the pie from the pan later.

Remove the two discs of Savory Pie Dough from the refrigerator. Cut one of the discs in half, and return one half-disc to the refrigerator. Add the other half-disc to the whole disc and leave them to soften on the counter for about 10 minutes. Softening the dough helps the two pieces combine, but if they aren't quite coming together, leave them for a few minutes longer to soften more.

Roll out the dough to a 13 x 16–inch (33 x 41–cm) rectangle, approximately ¼ inch (6 mm) thick.

Fit the dough to the loaf pan, following the technique in the Lining a Pie Plate or Tin section on pages 170 and 171. Trim the overhang to 1 inch (3 cm) beyond the rim of the loaf pan. Use a scrap piece of pie dough dipped in flour to press the dough into the corners of the pan. Look for holes and/or cracks and repair them, if necessary, by patching with scrap pieces of dough. Gather the leftover dough scraps together and set aside. Place the lined loaf pan in the refrigerator to firm up while you make the twists and decorations.

Make the Twists and Decorations

Line a baking sheet with parchment paper and set aside. Remove the other half-disc of dough from the refrigerator. Add the scraps from the first disc to the bottom of this disc and roll the dough out to a 10 x 10–inch (25 x 25–cm) square, about ⅛ inch (3 mm) thick. With a lattice cutter or a sharp knife and ruler, cut twenty-eight ¼ x 10–inch (6-mm x 25-cm) strands. Working with two strands at a time, make fourteen twists following the technique outlined in the Twist and Braiding Techniques section on pages 175 and 176. Place two of the twists on the baking sheet. Cut the other twelve twists in half to create twenty-four twists, each 5 inches (13 cm) in length. Place the twists on the baking sheet.

From the remaining rolled-out dough, cut an assortment of flower, leaf and butterfly cut-outs. (Depending on the size of the cutouts, you will need 16 to 24 in total.) Place these on the baking sheet. Transfer the baking sheet to the refrigerator.

(Continued)

Sometimes called Pizza Rustica, this classic Italian Easter Pie can only be described as a quiche on steroids. Packed with Italian meats mixed with two types of cheese and bound with eggs, this stunner of a pie is traditionally served to celebrate the end of Lent. Here, I've created a woven Easter basket and spring flowers design to welcome the first signs of spring after a long winter.

Makes one 5 x 9–inch (13 x 23–cm) rectangular pie

2 discs Savory Pie Dough (page 21)

1 red bell pepper, cut in half and deseeded

1 tsp olive oil

6 oz (170 g) Italian sausage, casings removed

4 large eggs, divided

10 oz (284 g) high-quality ricotta cheese (either homemade or store-bought)

6 oz (170 g) mozzarella cheese, cut into ½-inch (13-mm) cubes

6 oz (170 g) smoked ham, cubed

6 oz (170 g) sopressata or Genoa salami

1 tsp milk

3 oz (85 g) prosciutto

2 (10-oz [284-g]) packages frozen spinach, thawed and thoroughly squeezed to remove excess water

Easter Basket Pizza Pie
(Continued)

Make the Filling

Preheat the oven to 400°F (205°C). Line a baking sheet with tinfoil. Place the red bell pepper halves on the tinfoil-lined sheet and roast for 20 minutes, until soft and charred. Let the peppers cool, peel off the skin and slice each half into ¼-inch (6-mm) slices.

Heat the olive oil in a large skillet over medium heat. Add the sausage and cook, using a wooden spoon to break up any lumps, until no pink remains, approximately 8 minutes. Transfer the sausage to a small bowl and set aside to cool.

In a large bowl, whisk together three of the eggs. Stir in the ricotta and mozzarella. Add the smoked ham and sopressata. Set the bowl aside.

Assemble the Pie

In a small bowl, whisk together one egg and the milk to make the egg wash. Set aside.

Adjust the oven rack to the lower-middle position and place a baking sheet on it. Preheat the oven to 425°F (220°C). Remove the shell from the refrigerator. Lay three strips of prosciutto across the base of the shell. Sprinkle the sausage on top in an even layer. Cover the sausage with half of the spinach followed by half of the sliced red bell pepper. Spoon the egg–meat mixture over the spinach–red pepper mixture and smooth it with an offset spatula. Spread the remaining spinach over the filling, then lay in the remaining red bell pepper slices. Cover with the rest of the prosciutto.

Fold the pie dough overhang in and over the prosciutto (photo A).

Remove the tray of twists and decorations from the refrigerator. Lay the 5-inch (13-cm) twists across the 5-inch (13-cm) width of the pan, tightly butting them up against one another (photo B). When they are in position, take a sharp knife and trim the edges to the inside edge of the loaf pan. Apply egg wash to the twists. To create a neat edge to the pie, place a 10-inch (25-cm) twist down both sides of the pan and press lightly to adhere to the egg wash. Trim the twist ends to the edge of the pan.

Using the main photo as your guide, arrange the flowers, leaves and butterflies down the center top of the pie. Brush them with some additional egg wash. Place the pie in the freezer for 30 minutes.

(Continued)

Equipment

5 x 9–inch (13 x 23–cm) loaf pan, 2.75 inches (7 cm) deep

Lattice cutter

1-inch (3-cm) spring flower cutter

2-inch (5-cm) spring flower cutter

1-inch (3-cm) leaf cutter

2-inch (5-cm) leaf cutter

1-inch (3-cm) butterfly cutter

2-inch (5-cm) butterfly cutter

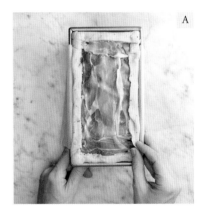

A

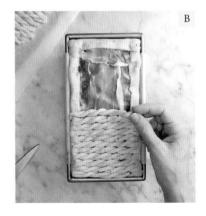

B

Easter Basket Pizza Pie
(Continued)

Bake the Pie

Place the pie on the preheated baking sheet in the oven and bake for 15 minutes at 425°F (220°C). Lower the temperature to 350°F (175°C) and continue to bake for another 45 minutes, or until the pie reaches an internal temperature of 165°F (75°C). Remove the pie from the oven and allow it to set for at least 3 hours. To remove the pie from the loaf pan, run a small offset spatula around the edges of the pie. Then, using the parchment paper as "handles," gently lift the pie from the loaf pan and slide onto a serving plate. Serve at room temperature or rewarm on a baking sheet, uncovered, in a 350°F (175°C) oven for 15 minutes.

To Make Ahead or Store

The pie can be made 1 day ahead and then reheated in a 300°F (150°C) oven or served at room temperature. Leftovers can be stored, covered, in the refrigerator for up to 3 days.

Valentine's Chocolate Box Strawberry Pie (page 149)

chapter 7

Next-Level Pies

From beautiful pastry florals and braids to the pastry fish scales on the Salmon Wellington (page 152), this wonderfully over-the-top collection of pies is designed to push the limits of your decorating talents to the next level. The payoff is extravagant pies that are sure to wow your guests and give you a huge sense of accomplishment.

A few words to the wise before you dive into this chapter. Each of these recipes will take time to make and decorate. For that reason, I encourage you to carefully read through the directions in advance and then divide the steps up over a few days if possible. For example, if the recipe calls for multiple batches of dough, make the discs a day or two in advance and keep them stored in the refrigerator. Decorations and pie shells can also be held in the refrigerator for up to 48 hours provided they are tightly covered. Also, keep in mind that the fillings used in the recipes in this chapter can easily be subbed in and out with others in the book if you prefer.

Spring Has Sprung
Apple-Rhubarb Pie

Featured Decorations: Embossed Lattice, Pie Dough Flowers & Braids

Prepare the Shell
Remove one disc of the Everyday All-Butter Pie Dough from the refrigerator. On a lightly floured surface, roll it out to a 12-inch (30-cm) circle. Gently transfer and fit the dough to the pie plate, following the directions in the Lining a Pie Plate or Tin section on pages 170 and 171, and leaving a ½-inch (13-mm) overhang. Gather up any leftover scraps and set aside. Place the pie shell in the refrigerator.

Make the Lattice Strips and Braids
Line a baking sheet with parchment paper and set aside. Remove the second disc of the Everyday All-Butter Pie Dough from the refrigerator. On a lightly floured surface, roll the dough out to a 12 x 14–inch (30 x 36–cm) rectangle. Using a sharp knife and a ruler, cut the rectangle in half to form two 12 x 7½–inch (30 x 19–cm) strips of dough. Emboss one of the strips with the lace impression mat, following the technique in the Embossing Pie Dough section on page 174. Cut the embossed dough into five 1½ x 12–inch (4 x 30–cm) strips and place them on the baking sheet.

From the remaining rolled dough, use a crimper roller to cut four ½ x 12–inch (13-mm x 30-cm) strips of dough. Add them to the baking sheet.

Using a sharp knife, cut eight ½ x 12–inch (13-mm x 30-cm) strips of dough. From these, make four 2-strand braids following the Two-Strand Braid directions in the Twist and Braiding Techniques section on page 175. Add the finished braids to the baking sheet and place it in the refrigerator.

Create and Assemble the Open Flowers
In a small bowl, whisk together the egg and milk to make the egg wash. Set aside.

Line a second baking sheet with parchment paper. Remove the third disc of Everyday All-Butter Pie Dough from the refrigerator. On a lightly floured surface, roll it out to a 12-inch (30-cm) square. Using the 1½-inch (4-cm) five-petal cutter, cut twelve flowers. Using the 2-inch (5-cm) five-petal cutter, cut 24 flowers. Place the rest of the rolled-out dough back in the refrigerator. Working with one flower at a time on the nonstick mat, roll the ball tool around the petal edges to thin and feather them. Place the flowers on the baking sheet.

(Continued)

I've always been fascinated by those amazing sugar flowers on high-end cake designs. I wondered whether the technique used to create those beautiful petals would translate to a pastry format. After investing in a few inexpensive fondant tools, and watching more than a few YouTube tutorials, the answer is a resounding "yes!" This pie would be a beautiful addition to a bridal shower or wedding dinner.

Makes one double-crust, 9-inch (23-cm) round pie

3 discs Everyday All-Butter Pie Dough (page 21), chilled

1 large egg

1 tsp milk

2 lb (907 g) apples (Gala, Spy, Cortland, Golden Delicious or a mix), peeled, cored and cut into ¼-inch (6-mm) slices

2 cups (245 g) sliced rhubarb (½-inch [13-mm] pieces), fresh or frozen (defrosted)

1 tbsp (15 ml) fresh lemon juice

¾ cup (150 g) granulated sugar

¼ cup (32 g) tapioca starch or cornstarch

½ tsp cinnamon

¼ tsp kosher salt

Spring Has Sprung Apple-Rhubarb Pie (Continued)

To assemble the flowers, place one of the 2-inch (5-cm) feathered flowers on a flat surface. Dab the center of the flower with a little egg wash. Place another 2-inch (5-cm) feathered flower on top of it, offsetting it slightly. Dab a little egg wash on the center of this flower. Place a 1½-inch (4-cm) feathered flower on top, offsetting it slightly.

Pick up the assembled flower and pinch the base to hold the petals together. Use the base of the ball tool to make an indentation in the middle of the flower (photo A).

From the scraps of pie dough, roll pea-sized balls and fit them into the middle of each flower. Place your finished flowers on the baking sheet. You will have 12 flowers.

Create and Assemble the Closed Flowers
Roll out the remaining dough scraps to a ⅛-inch (3-mm) thickness. To create a closed flower, cut twenty-four 1-inch (3-cm), five-petal flowers. Working with one flower at a time, dab the middle of the flower with egg wash. Place a second flower on top of it, offsetting the petals. Roll a pea-sized ball of dough and place it in the center of the flower (photo B).

Holding the flower in your hands, push up on the petals so they form around the ball. Repeat this technique to make twelve closed flowers. Place the finished flowers on the baking sheet with the open flowers and transfer it to the refrigerator.

Make the Filling
In a large saucepan or a Dutch oven, toss the apples, rhubarb, lemon juice, sugar, tapioca starch or cornstarch, cinnamon and salt until thoroughly combined. Cook over medium heat, stirring frequently, until the apples have softened and the liquid has thickened (6 to 8 minutes). Transfer the filling to a rimmed baking sheet and allow it to cool to room temperature, 20 to 30 minutes.

(Continued)

Equipment
Standard 9-inch (23-cm) pie plate, about 1¾ inches (4.5 cm) deep

Ruler

Impression mat with lace design

Crimped pastry wheel

1½-inch (4-cm) five-petal cutter

2-inch (5-cm) five-petal cutter

Ball tool

1-inch (3-cm) five-petal cutter

Square of nonstick foam

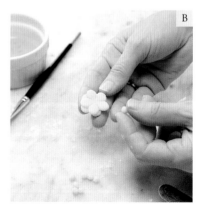

Spring Has Sprung Apple–Rhubarb Pie (Continued)

Assemble the Pie

Adjust the oven rack to the lower-middle position and place a baking sheet on it. Preheat the oven to 425°F (220°C). Remove the baking sheet with the lattice strips from the refrigerator. On a piece of parchment paper, mark a 9-inch (23-cm) circle with a marker or pencil. Turn the parchment paper over, ensuring the mark can be seen through the paper. Starting at the left side of the marked surface, evenly space across the pie (in this order) a crimped strip, an embossed strip, a braid, a crimped strip, an embossed strip and a braid. Next, lay your horizontal lattice strips in the following order: embossed strip, braid, crimped strip, embossed strip, crimped strip, braid and embossed strip following the latticing technique in the Latticing a Pie section on pages 177 and 178 (photo C).

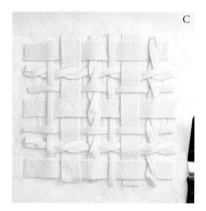

When you are happy with the placement, transfer the lattice, on the parchment, to a baking sheet and freeze for 15 minutes.

Remove the pie shell from the refrigerator and spoon the cooled filling into it. Brush the edges of the pie with egg wash. Remove the lattice top from the freezer. Slide a pizza lifter or large spatula under the lattice and gently move it onto the prepared pie shell. Leave the lattice to warm for about 5 minutes and then trim the edges back with scissors or a knife to a ½-inch (13-mm) overhang (photo D).

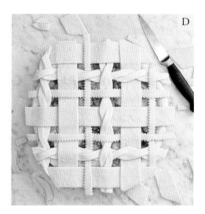

Wrap the lattice strips around the edge of the pie plate and trim further to fit snugly, if necessary. Using the unbaked pie photo (page 144) as a guide, place the open and closed flowers decoratively in a half-moon pattern around the pie, dabbing egg wash to secure them to the pie top. Move the finished pie to the freezer for 30 minutes.

Bake the Pie

Carefully brush the entire pie with egg wash. Place the pie in the oven on the preheated baking sheet and bake at 425°F (220°C) for 15 minutes. Reduce the heat to 375°F (190°C) and bake for another 50 to 60 minutes, or until the filling bubbles in the center of the pie. If the flowers begin to brown too quickly, cover them with tinfoil. Allow the pie to rest for at least 3 hours so the filling can set before serving.

To Make Ahead or Store

The pie can be baked 1 day ahead and stored at room temperature, loosely covered. Leftover pie can be covered and stored at room temperature for up to 2 days.

The unbaked pie may be frozen, egg washed and double wrapped, for up to 3 months. It must be baked from frozen. You may need to add an additional 10 to 15 minutes to the baking time for frozen pies.

Valentine's Chocolate Box Strawberry Pie

Featured Decorations: Embossed Pie Dough, Pie Dough Roses

Create the Heart Pie Dough Top

In a small bowl, whisk together the egg and milk to make the egg wash. Set aside.

Remove one disc of the Everyday All-Butter Pie Dough from the refrigerator. On a lightly floured piece of parchment paper, roll out the dough to a 12-inch (30-cm) square, about ⅛ inch (3 mm) thick. Using a rolling pin and impression mat, emboss the dough with a decorative impression mat of your choice (the one used for this design is a lace design), following the technique in the Embossing Pie Dough section on page 174. Flip the top of the tart tin over and press it down firmly on the dough to make a heart cutout (photo A).

Slide the heart, on the parchment paper, onto a baking sheet and transfer it to the refrigerator. Set the leftover dough aside.

Line a baking sheet with parchment paper and set aside. Remove the second disc of Everyday All-Butter Pie Dough from the refrigerator. Add the scraps from the first dough disc to the bottom of this disc. Roll the dough out to a 12 x 14–inch (30 x 36–cm) rectangle. Cut a 12 x 4–inch (30 x 10–cm) strip and, using a rolling pin and impression mat, emboss the dough with the same impression mat you used for the heart shape. Cut the embossed strip into four 12 x 1–inch (30 x 3–cm) ribbons and place on the baking sheet. With the remaining dough, cut as many 1½-inch (4-cm) rounds as you can for the pie dough roses, rerolling the dough as necessary to cut more. Place the rounds on the baking sheet.

(Continued)

When I was a teenager, I would dream about receiving one of those satin and lace–covered drugstore boxes of chocolates on Valentine's Day. I must admit, I still get a bit nostalgic when I see a heart-shaped box of chocolates, which is why it was the first thing that came to mind when I decided to design a Valentine's Day–themed pie. You won't find any chocolates inside this one, but I promise you the strawberry filling is a fine substitute.

Makes one double-crust, 9-inch (23-cm) heart-shaped pie

1 large egg

1 tsp milk

4 discs Everyday All-Butter Pie Dough (page 21)

½ cup (100 g) granulated sugar

¼ cup (32 g) tapioca starch or cornstarch

Pinch of kosher salt

2½ lb (1.1 kg) fresh strawberries, cored, hulled and quartered

Equipment

Impression mat

9-inch (23-cm) heart-shaped tart tin with removable bottom

1½-inch (4-cm) circle cutter

2½-inch (6.5-cm) circle cutter, optional

1-inch (3-cm) daisy cutter

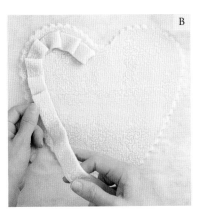

Valentine's Chocolate Box Strawberry Pie (Continued)

Remove the embossed pie dough heart from the refrigerator and brush some egg wash along the border. To apply the embossed ribbon, fold the dough ribbon strips back over themselves approximately every 1 inch (3 cm) (photo B [page 149]). You will need two strips for each side of the heart. Hide any areas where the strips join under a fold. Return the dough heart, on the baking sheet, to the refrigerator.

Remove the third disc of Everyday All-Butter Pie Dough from the refrigerator. On a lightly floured surface, roll out the dough to a 12-inch (30-cm) circle. Using the 1½-inch (4-cm) circle cutter, cut as many rounds as you can from the dough, rerolling as necessary to create more. Use these rounds, along with the ones already on your baking sheet, to create pie dough roses, following the technique in the Climbing Roses Peach Slab Pie recipe on pages 30 to 34. Your roses can all be one size (using five rounds), or you can add more rounds to make bigger roses or fewer rounds to make smaller rosebuds. If you wish to create a large rose in the center, use a 2½-inch (6.5-cm) circle cutter and cut twelve rounds.

Remove the pie dough heart from the refrigerator. Brush the center with some egg wash and place the roses tightly within the "ribbon" border. Using the small daisy cutter, cut sixteen 1-inch (3-cm) daisies and place them decoratively over the roses. Freeze the finished pie top on the baking sheet for 15 minutes.

Make the Filling and Pie Shell
In a small bowl, whisk together the sugar, tapioca starch or cornstarch and salt. Place the strawberries in a large bowl. Sprinkle the sugar-starch mixture over the strawberries and toss gently until evenly coated. Set aside.

To make the pie shell, roll out the fourth disc of Everyday All-Butter Pie Dough to a 12-inch (30-cm) square. Transfer and fit the dough to the tart tin following the directions in the Lining a Pie Plate or Tin section on pages 170 and 171, and trim to the edge of the tin.

Assemble the Pie
Adjust the oven rack to the lower-middle position and place a baking sheet on it. Preheat the oven to 425°F (220°C). Spoon the strawberry mixture into the pie shell. Brush the edges of the pie shell with some egg wash. Remove the heart top from the freezer. Slide a pizza lifter or large spatula under it and gently move it onto the prepared pie shell. Press down around the edges to adhere it to the shell. Using a sharp knife, cut vents between several of the roses. Brush the top of the pie with egg wash.

Bake the Pie
Transfer the pie to the preheated baking sheet in the oven. Bake for 15 minutes at 425°F (220°C) and then lower the temperature to 375°F (190°C). Bake for another 50 to 60 minutes, until the top of the pie is golden brown and the strawberry filling starts to bubble up between the roses. Cover the top loosely with tinfoil if it browns too quickly. Allow the pie to cool for at least 3 hours before serving.

To Make Ahead or Store
The pie can be baked 1 day ahead and stored at room temperature, loosely covered. Leftover pie can be covered and stored at room temperature for up to 2 days. The unbaked pie may be frozen, egg washed and double wrapped, for up to 3 months. It must be baked from frozen. You may need to add an additional 10 to 15 minutes to the baking time for frozen pies.

See baked photo on page 142.

Salmon Wellington

Featured Decorations: Pastry Fish, Braids

Make the Spinach-Leek Filling
Melt the butter in a large skillet over medium-low heat. Add the leeks and sauté until soft, 6 to 8 minutes, stirring occasionally. Add the spinach and 1 tablespoon (1 g) of the dill and continue sautéing until the spinach has wilted and any liquid has been absorbed, about 3 minutes. Season with the salt and pepper. Set the filling aside to cool.

Make the Dill Sauce
Combine the yogurt, mayonnaise, 1 tablespoon (1 g) of the dill, lemon juice and garlic in a small bowl. Keep refrigerated until ready to use.

Assemble the Salmon
In a small bowl, whisk together the egg and milk to make the egg wash. Set aside.

Adjust the oven rack to the lower-middle position. Preheat the oven to 425°F (220°C).

On a cutting board, use a sharp knife to trim the salmon fillet to form the rough shape of the fish head and trunk (the tail will be made out of pastry only). The trimmed piece of salmon should be approximately 5 x 11 inches (13 x 28 cm). Line a large baking sheet with parchment paper. Remove one sheet of puff pastry from the refrigerator and lay it on the baking sheet, with the long edge facing you. Position the salmon fillet on the puff pastry, ensuring that you have at least 1 inch (3 cm) of pastry above the head, 3 inches (8 cm) beyond the torso (for the tail) and 1 inch (3 cm) on each side of the fish (photo A). Do not trim the puff pastry yet. Brush some egg wash around the shape of the fish on the pastry.

(Continued)

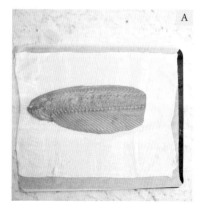
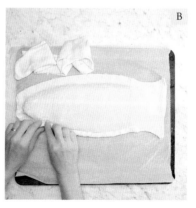

This showstopper dish combines tender salmon topped with a fresh spinach and leek filling wrapped in a flaky, golden puff pastry. And because I can never seem to leave well enough alone, I made it in the shape of a fish, scales and all. I think I must have been channeling my inner Mrs. Patmore from Downton Abbey *on this one. Serve it with a yogurt-dill sauce and wait for the accolades.*

Serves eight

2 tbsp (30 g) unsalted butter

2 leeks, washed and thinly sliced

4 cups (120 g) spinach, roughly chopped

2 tbsp (2 g) fresh dill, chopped, divided

1 tsp kosher salt

½ tsp pepper

1 cup (245 g) plain Greek-style yogurt

¼ cup (60 g) mayonnaise

1 tsp fresh lemon juice

1 tsp minced garlic

1 large egg

1 tsp milk

3 lb (1.3 kg) boneless salmon fillet, skinned

3 (10 x 15–inch [25 x 38–cm]) sheets, pre-rolled frozen puff pastry, thawed

Equipment
¾-inch (2-cm) circle cutter or
¾-inch (2-cm) plain piping tip

Salmon Wellington (Continued)

Spread the spinach-leek filling evenly over the top of the salmon fillet. Remove the second sheet of puff pastry from the refrigerator and lay it over the salmon and filling. Using a sharp knife, cut the pastry into a fish shape, following the lines of the salmon fillet, leaving a 1-inch (3-cm) border around the top and sides of the fish and making a 3-inch (8-cm) fanned tail outline. Gather the leftover scraps of puff pastry together and cover with plastic wrap to keep them from drying out. Gently press all around the fish shape to seal the two pieces of puff pastry together (photo B [page 152]).

Roll the 1-inch (3-cm) pastry border under itself to tuck it in, pressing firmly and following the outline of the fish head, body and tail. You should now have a ½-inch (13-mm) border all the way around the fish. With a sharp knife, cut vents down the body of the fish (photo C).

Decorate the Salmon
Using a knife, create horizontal markings along the fish tail (photo D).

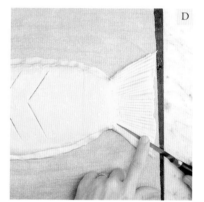

Remove the third sheet of puff pastry from the refrigerator. Using a ¾-inch (2-cm) circle cutter or the top of a plain ¾-inch (2-cm) pastry tip, cut approximately 180 circles, rerolling the puff pastry if necessary. Brush the trunk of the fish with egg wash. Starting at the base of the tail, create rows of overlapping circles, offsetting every other row as you move toward the neck, to create the appearance of scales (photo E). Stop the scales when you reach the base of the fish neck.

For the face, roll a small piece of dough for the eye of the fish. To create the mouth, use your thumb to indent the pastry and mold the pastry with your fingers to create the shape.

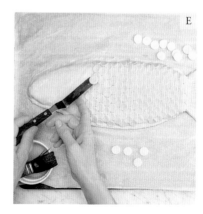

Roll out the leftover scraps of puff pastry to a ⅛-inch (3-mm) thickness. Cut twelve ¼ x 6–inch (6-mm x 15-cm) pastry strands and make six 2-strand braids, following the Two-Strand Braid directions outlined in the Twist and Braiding Techniques section on page 175. Apply some egg wash to the border of the fish and attach the braids around the trunk and head of the fish dabbing a bit of egg wash at the end of each strand as you connect it to the next. Place one braid across the base of the fish head to separate it from the fish scales.

Brush the entire fish gently with the remaining egg wash. Transfer the fish, on the parchment-lined baking sheet, to the oven and bake for 25 minutes, or until a thermometer registers 145°F (65°C) when it is gently inserted into the thickest part of the fish and the pastry is golden brown. Allow the fish to rest for at least 15 minutes before cutting. Serve warm or at room temperature with the yogurt-dill dressing on the side.

To Make Ahead or Store
The Wellington can be assembled 1 day ahead and stored in the refrigerator, tightly covered. Leftover Wellington can be covered and stored in the refrigerator for up to 2 days.

Apple-Cranberry Winter Wreath Pie

Featured Decorations: Pie Dough Pinecones, Branches, Holly, Ribbon & Bow

Make the Apple Filling

In a small bowl, stir together the brown sugar, 3 tablespoons (24 g) of the tapioca or cornstarch, ground cinnamon, nutmeg, allspice and salt. Place the apple slices in a large bowl and sprinkle the sugar mixture over them. Toss to combine. Set aside.

Make the Cranberry Filling

In a small bowl, combine the cranberries, granulated sugar and 1 tablespoon (8 g) of the tapioca or cornstarch. Set aside.

Make the Wreath

Remove one disc of the Everyday All-Butter Pie Dough from the refrigerator. On a lightly floured piece of parchment paper, roll out the dough to a 12-inch (30-cm) circle. Turn the pie plate upside down on the dough. Score the outline of the plate lightly with a sharp knife (do not cut through), then cut a circle that is 1 inch (3 cm) wider than the diameter (giving you a 10-inch [25-cm] circle). Using the 5-inch (13-cm) rim of a bowl or a 5-inch (13-cm) circle cutter, cut a circle in the center of the dough circle. Slide the parchment, with the circle wreath on it, onto a baking sheet and place it in the refrigerator. Gather the leftover scraps of dough and return them to the refrigerator.

Prepare the Shell

Remove the second disc of the Everyday All-Butter Pie Dough from the refrigerator. Roll out the dough to a 12-inch (30-cm) round. Transfer and fit the dough to the pie plate, following the directions in the Lining a Pie Plate or Tin on pages 170 and 171, leaving a ½-inch (13-mm) overhang. Transfer the dough-lined plate to the refrigerator.

Make the Pastry Pinecones

Line a baking sheet with parchment paper and set aside. Retrieve the leftover dough scraps from the refrigerator and add them to the scraps from the pie shell. From the leftover scraps, pull off twelve walnut-sized pieces of dough. Roll each piece into a log shape, between ½ inch (13 mm) and 1 inch (3 cm) in length. Make each log slightly wider at the top than the bottom so that it resembles a pinecone. Place the logs on the baking sheet and put them in the freezer for 5 minutes to firm up.

(Continued)

This gorgeous pie combines two of my favorite flavors—cranberries and apples. It's an easy filling to make, which is a good thing because you're going to have to set aside a wee bit of time to get this pie decorated. But, believe me, it's going to be worth it when the choirs of heavenly angels herald its arrival at the holiday dinner table.

Makes one 9-inch (23-cm), double-crust round pie

½ cup (110 g) brown sugar

4 tbsp (32 g) tapioca flour or cornstarch, divided

1 tsp ground cinnamon

½ tsp nutmeg

¼ tsp allspice

Dash of kosher salt

2 lb (907 g) apples (Gala, Spy Cortland, Golden Delicious or a mix), peeled, cored and cut into ¼-inch (6-mm) slices

1 cup (100 g) fresh cranberries

¼ cup (50 g) granulated sugar

3 discs Everyday All-Butter Pie Dough (page 21)

1 large egg

1 tsp milk

Equipment

9-inch (23-cm) round standard pie plate

5-inch (13-cm) circle cutter

Crimper

½-inch (13-mm) holly leaf cutter

1-inch (3-cm) holly leaf cutter

Apple-Cranberry Winter Wreath Pie (Continued)

Working with one log at a time, place the tip of a small rounded spoon against the edge of the pinecone to create a row of semi-circle impressions across the top of the pinecone. On the next row, place the semi-circle impressions between the impressions of the first row. Continue this process down the length of the pinecone, alternating rows as you go (photo A). Place the finished pine cones on the baking sheet.

A

Make the Fir Branches
Remove the third disc of Everyday All-Butter Pie Dough from the refrigerator. Pull twelve walnut-sized pieces of dough from the disc. With the palm of your hand, roll each one into a long, narrow tube. Laying each one flat on a lightly floured surface, use a sharp knife to make diagonal incisions down both sides of the tube to make the fir needles (photo B). Repeat this process until you have twelve fir branches. Add the branches to the baking sheet with the pinecones. Set aside.

Make the Bow and Ribbon
In a small bowl, whisk together the egg and milk to make the egg wash. Set aside.

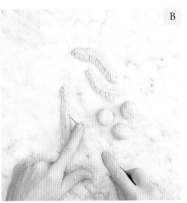

B

Line a baking sheet with parchment paper and set aside. On a lightly floured surface, roll out the remainder of the dough to a 4 x 12–inch (10 x 30–cm) rectangle. Using a ruler and a sharp knife, cut one 1 x 12–inch (3 x 30–cm) strip of dough. Using a crimper, lightly roll a line down each side of the strip.

Turn the strip over. Place a dab of water at the center point of the strip. Fold both ends of the strip toward the middle so that they meet. Press down lightly on the seam (photo C).

Cut one 1 x 2–inch (3 x 5–cm) piece of dough from the remaining dough. Roll a crimp line down the center of the strip. Wrap it carefully around the center of the bow to neatly cover the seam.

With your fingers, reach into the loops and make small folds and bends in the ribbon to create a realistic effect.

(Continued)

C

Apple-Cranberry Winter Wreath Pie (Continued)

Cut one 1 x 8–inch (3 x 20–cm) strip of dough. Run a crimp line down the center of the strip. Cut the strip in half so you have two 1 x 4–inch (3 x 10–cm) pieces of dough. Cut a "V" shape in the end of each piece (photo D). Move the pieces to the baking sheet and place them together in an upside-down V shape (photo E). Dab a little water to secure the two pieces together at the top. Then, dab a little water on top of the assembled "V" shape and gently move the assembled bow so that it sits on top of the inverted V-shaped ribbon. Press gently to adhere. To create folds in the ribbon, roll up small pieces of scrap dough and place them within the bow loops and ribbon (photo F). Place the baking sheet with the assembled bow on it in the freezer for 5 minutes to firm up.

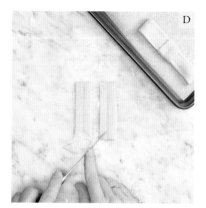

Make the Holly Leaves and Berries

Reroll the remaining scraps of the dough to an ⅛-inch (3-mm) thickness. Using the ½-inch (13-mm) and 1-inch (3-cm) holly leaf cutters, cut approximately twenty holly leaves. From dough scraps, roll up little balls of various sizes. You will need 30 to 40 holly berries. Add the holly leaves and berries to the baking sheet with the fir branches.

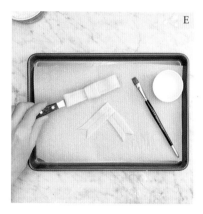

Assemble the Decorations

Remove the pie dough wreath circle from the refrigerator and brush it with some egg wash. Place the fir branches decoratively around the wreath, bending and turning them to give them dimension, being careful to stay within the scored border that you made. Leave some space at the top of the wreath undecorated. This is where the bow will go. Next, place the holly leaves in and around the fir branches, tucking them in here and there, and bending them to give them shape and dimension. Scatter the holly berries decoratively around the wreath.

Place the pinecones in groups of two or three around the wreath, tucking them between the holly leaves and fir branches. Dab the spot where the bow will go with some egg wash. Remove the bow from the freezer and carefully place it at the top of the wreath. Use any leftover fir and holly leaves to fill in any bald spots. Place the wreath in the freezer for 15 minutes to firm up.

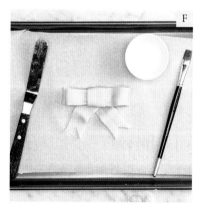

(Continued)

Apple-Cranberry Winter Wreath Pie (Continued)

Assemble the Pie

Adjust the oven rack to the lower-middle position and place a baking sheet on it. Preheat the oven to 425°F (220°C). Remove the chilled pie shell from the refrigerator. Spoon the apple filling into the shell in an even layer, laying the apples flat and packing them tightly together. Spoon the cranberry filling mixture on top and smooth it with an offset spatula, covering the apple filling entirely.

Brush the edges of the pie with egg wash. Remove the wreath pie top from the freezer. Slide a pizza lifter or large spatula under the wreath and gently move it onto the prepared pie shell. Position it so that the center lines up with the center of the pie. Use a sharp knife to cut away the excess pie dough around the edges of the pie. Gently press on the edges of the pie top to adhere it to the bottom. Use egg wash and a soft pastry brush (or paint brush) to cover the pie in egg wash. Place the decorated pie on a baking sheet and transfer it to the oven.

Bake the Pie

Bake the pie for 15 minutes at 425°F (220°C), then turn the oven down to 375°F (190°C) and continue baking for another 50 to 60 minutes. If the wreath begins to brown too quickly, cover it with a sheet of tinfoil. To prevent the cranberries from burning, turn them gently halfway during baking or cover them with a circle of tinfoil. The pie is done when it is nicely browned and the filling in the center is bubbling. Allow the pie to cool for at least 3 hours before serving.

To Make Ahead or Store

The pie can be baked 1 day ahead and stored at room temperature, loosely covered. Leftover pie can be covered and stored at room temperature for up to 2 days.

The unbaked pie may be frozen, egg washed and double wrapped, for up to 3 months. It must be baked from frozen. You may need to add an additional 10 to 15 minutes to the baking time for frozen pies.

Lemon-Blueberry Dahlias Pie

Featured Decorations: Pie Dough Dahlias, Braids

Make the Base for the Pie Top

Remove one disc of the Everyday All-Butter Pie Dough from the refrigerator. On a piece of lightly floured parchment paper, roll it out to a 12-inch (30-cm) circle, about ⅛ inch (3 mm) thick.

Turn the tart tin upside down and press it down lightly on the dough to leave an outline of the pan, being careful not to cut all the way through the dough. Using a knife, cut a circle 1 inch (3 cm) beyond this mark all around the dough impression. Slide the parchment, with the dough circle on it, onto a baking sheet and transfer it to the refrigerator. Save the dough scraps for the next step.

Make the Pie Shell

Remove the second disc of Everyday All-Butter Pie Dough from the refrigerator. Add the leftover dough scraps from the first disc to the bottom of this disc. On a lightly floured surface, roll it out to a 12-inch (30-cm) circle. Gently transfer the dough to the tart tin, following the directions in the Lining a Pie Plate or Tin section on pages 170 and 171, and leaving a ½-inch (13-mm) overhang. Transfer the dough-lined tart tin to the refrigerator. Save the dough scraps for the next step.

Make the Decorative Strips

Remove the third disc of Everyday All-Butter Pie Dough from the refrigerator. Add any leftover dough scraps from the second disc to the bottom of this disc. On a lightly floured piece of parchment paper, roll the dough out to a 12 x 14–inch (30 x 36–cm) rectangle, about ⅛ inch (3 mm) thick. Using a sharp knife and ruler, or a lattice cutter, cut twenty-eight ½ x 12–inch (13-mm x 30-cm) strips of pie dough. Slide the parchment, with the dough strips on it, onto a baking sheet and set aside. Save the dough scraps for the next step.

Remove the fourth disc of Everyday All-Butter Pie Dough from the refrigerator. Add any leftover dough scraps from the third disc to the bottom of this disc. On a lightly floured surface, roll the dough out to a 10 x 14–inch (25 x 36–cm) rectangle, about ⅛ inch (3 mm) thick. Using a sharp knife and ruler, or a lattice cutter, cut eighteen ½ x 14–inch (13-mm x 36-cm) strips of dough. Using two strips at a time, make nine twists following the directions outlined in the Twist and Braiding Techniques section on pages 175 and 176. Gently transfer the twists to the baking sheet. Set the baking sheet aside.

(Continued)

Dahlias have always been among my favorite flowers. I love their elegance, showiness and versatility. This pie showcases their sculptural beauty to full effect. I've chosen a two-tone pastry here to tie in with the lemon-blueberry filling, but you could make this pie top as a single color and it would still look fabulous. Just like the dahlia herself.

Makes one 9-inch (23-cm) round double-crust pie

5 discs Everyday All-Butter Pie Dough (page 21), chilled

1 large egg

1 tsp milk

1 disc Deep Purple Blueberry Pie Dough (page 27), chilled

5½ cups (815 g) blueberries, washed and picked over

¾ cup (150 g) granulated sugar

1 tbsp (15 ml) lemon juice

1 tsp lemon zest

⅓ cup (42 g) tapioca starch or cornstarch

½ tsp kosher salt

Equipment

9-inch (23-cm) round tart tin with removable bottom

Lattice cutter

1-inch (3-cm) flower cutter

½-inch (13-mm) flower cutter

1-inch (3-cm) circle cutter

1-inch (3-cm) square cutter

1½-inch (4-cm) square cutter

1½-inch (4-cm) leaf cutter

1-inch (3-cm) leaf cutter

Lemon–Blueberry Dahlias Pie
(Continued)

In a small bowl, whisk together the egg and milk to make the egg wash. Set aside.

Remove the baking sheet containing the dough circle from the refrigerator. Using a pastry brush, brush the surface of the round with some egg wash. Take two flat dough strips from your other baking sheet and lay them vertically, side by side, on the left edge of the round. They will extend over the edge of the circle (you'll trim these later). Place a dough twist next to the pair of flat strips. Repeat this pattern across the dough circle, alternating twists and pairs of flat strips, until you've completely covered the dough circle. Return the covered dough circle on the baking sheet to the refrigerator.

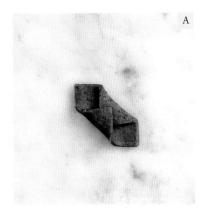

Make the Flowers
Set the now empty baking sheet aside (leave the parchment on it). Remove the disc of Deep Purple Blueberry Pie Dough from the refrigerator. On a lightly floured surface, roll it to a 13-inch (33-cm) circle, about ⅛ inch (3 mm) thick. Using 1-inch (3-cm) and ½-inch (13-mm) flower cutters, cut twelve 1-inch (3-cm) flowers and twelve ½-inch (13-mm) flowers. Dab a little egg wash in the middle of the 1-inch (3-cm) flowers and then place the ½-inch (13-mm) flowers on top. Curl up the edges of the flowers. Use leftover scraps of either the blueberry or all-butter dough to roll small balls and place them in the center of each flower. Using an offset spatula, transfer the finished flowers to the baking sheet.

Make the Dahlia Petals
From the same piece of blueberry dough, cut four 1-inch (3-cm) circles, forty-two 1-inch (3-cm) squares and sixteen 1½-inch (4-cm) squares. For each square, fold the top right corner to the center. Dab some egg wash on the bottom left corner of the square and fold it toward the center, overlapping the other corner slightly (photo A).

Repeat this process to make petals from all the 1-inch (3-cm) and 1½-inch (4-cm) squares.

Assemble the Dahlias
To make the large blueberry dahlia, lay a 1-inch (3-cm) blueberry dough circle on a floured surface and add a dab of egg wash. Lay a circle of seven 1½-inch (4-cm) rolled petals around the circle (photo B).

Repeat the process for a second layer of seven 1½-inch (4-cm) petals, positioning them between the petals on the first layer.

Cut two rolled petals in half. Enclose the flower with four half-petals as a third layer (photo C).

Use an offset spatula to transfer the completed flower to the baking sheet.

(Continued)

Lemon-Blueberry Dahlias Pie
(Continued)

Using the same technique, build three small blueberry dahlias using a 1-inch (3-cm) circle as the base, with six 1-inch (3-cm) rolled petals on the first layer, six 1-inch (3-cm) petals on the second layer and four 1-inch (3-cm) half-petals on the third level. Use a small offset spatula to add these to the baking sheet with the other flower.

Remove the fifth disc of Everyday All-Butter Pie Dough from the refrigerator. On a lightly floured surface, roll it out to a 12-inch (30-cm) round, about ⅛ inch (3 mm) thick. Cut out four 1-inch (3-cm) circles, forty-eight 1½-inch (4-cm) squares and fourteen 1-inch (3-cm) squares. Follow the same technique used for the blueberry dahlias to create three large and one small dahlia. Set the completed dahlias on the baking sheet with the other flowers. Use the remaining all-butter pie dough to create eight 1½-inch (4-cm) leaves and four 1-inch (3-cm) leaves and add to the baking sheet. Place all the decorations in the refrigerator for 10 minutes.

Assemble the Pie
Remove the pie dough top and the decorations from the refrigerator. Using a sharp knife, cut away any overhang from the flat and twist strips so the strips are flush to the edge of the dough circle. Place the blueberry and all-butter dahlias decoratively around the pie top, using the photo on page 162 as your guide, and leaving a ½-inch (13-mm) border around the pie top. Tuck the leaves amongst the dahlias. If you have any dough left, create small flowers or cut more leaves to fill in any gaps. Place the pie top in the freezer for 30 minutes.

Adjust the oven rack to the lower-middle position and place a baking sheet on it. Preheat the oven to 425°F (220°C).

Make the Lemon-Blueberry Filling
In a large bowl, put the blueberries, sugar, lemon juice, lemon zest, tapioca starch or cornstarch and salt. With a wooden spoon, gently toss the ingredients until thoroughly combined. Set the bowl aside.

Remove the pie shell from the refrigerator and fill it with the lemon-blueberry filling. Brush the edges of the pie shell with egg wash. Remove the pie top from the freezer. Slide a pizza lifter or large spatula under the pie top and gently move it onto the prepared pie shell. Using a sharp knife, trim the excess dough so the top is flush to the outer edge of the pie plate. Press firmly down all around the edges of the pie to ensure that it is sealed.

Bake the Pie
Using a wooden skewer or sharp knife, poke vents amongst the flowers. Brush the entire pie with egg wash. Once again, press down all around the edges of the pie to ensure it is sealed. Place the finished pie in the oven on the preheated baking sheet, and bake for 15 minutes at 425°F (220°C). Reduce the oven to 375°F (190°C) and bake for another 50 to 60 minutes, until the pie is golden brown. Allow the pie to set by cooling it for at least 3 hours before serving.

To Make Ahead or Store
The pie can be baked 1 day ahead and stored at room temperature, loosely covered. Leftover pie can be covered and stored at room temperature for up to 2 days.

The unbaked pie may be frozen, egg washed and double wrapped, for up to 3 months. It must be baked from frozen. You may need to add an additional 10 to 15 minutes to the baking time for frozen pies.

chapter 8

Essential Pie Skills and Decorating Techniques

As with all types of baking, there are essential skills you should master before you bake a pie. This chapter covers those basics, from the best way to roll dough (page 168) and move it to a pie plate (page 170) to the proper steps to partial and full blind baking (page 172) and basic braiding, latticing and crimping techniques (page 175).

How you use the information within these pages will depend on your skill level. If are already familiar with the topics covered here, this chapter can serve as a quick read-through or a reference when you need it. If you are new to the world of pie making and decorating, on the other hand, you may want to take more time with it to ensure you are comfortable with the basics before proceeding. Either way, I hope you gain practical knowledge that makes the pie-making experience an enjoyable and rewarding one.

Rolling Out Pie Dough

Rolling out pie dough is one of those things that sounds simple in principle but can be a bit more challenging in practice. The good news is that there are lots of things you can do that will have you rocking (and rolling) your pie dough like a pro in no time.

Keep Your Pie Dough Cold
It may go without saying at this point, but I'm going to say it anyway. Your pie dough needs to be cold when you work with it. Pie dough that is not chilled enough will stick to your rolling pin, tear and generally make you miserable. Let's avoid that, shall we, by giving your pie dough the proper amount of time to rest and chill before you start working with it. Because most of the pie dough recipes in this book are butter based, you may need to give your dough disc 5 minutes on the counter after its resting time in the refrigerator to soften *a bit* so it's easier to roll.

Tip:
Always choose a flat rolling surface away from the heat of a stove or a dishwasher. If your kitchen is warm, it's better to work on parchment paper or a silicone mat rather than directly on a kitchen surface. That way, if your dough becomes too soft, you can easily slide it and the liner onto a baking sheet and return it to the refrigerator to firm up. In about 5 minutes you'll be back in business again.

Flour Your Rolling Pin and Surface

Contrary to what you may have heard, your pie dough is not a snowflake. It can stand up to a *bit* more extra flour. Your goal is to keep your dough moving on your surface and the only way to do that is to start with a lightly floured rolling pin and a lightly floured surface. As you roll, add more flour to your pin and/or work surface at the first sign of sticky dough.

Get Your Rolling Technique Down

Most pie dough will be rolled out into a circle. To get an evenly rolled, round pie dough sheet, start by placing your rolling pin in the center of the dough with your hands at 9 o'clock and 3 o'clock.

Using a light, even pressure, roll the pie dough from the center to the bottom edge (photo A). Return to the center position and roll the dough to the top edge. Lift a corner of the dough and sweep the dough across the floured surface to pick up a bit of flour as you turn it a quarter turn (photo B).

Repeat the rolling pattern. Continue turning and rolling until your dough is the size and thickness called for in the recipe, adding more flour to your rolling pin and throwing down a small amount of flour on the work surface when your dough stops moving or starts sticking. If the dough becomes very sticky and warm, place it on a parchment-lined baking sheet and return it to the refrigerator to chill for about 5 minutes.

Tips:

While keeping the dough moving in quarter-turns is the best way to roll out a dough circle, it can still get misshapen. If that happens, simply angle one end of your rolling pin in the direction of the area that needs filling in, then continue your rolling pattern.

In my opinion, the ideal thickness for rolled-out pie dough is ⅛ inch (3 mm). Pie dough that is thicker than that may not cook in the time stated in the recipe (especially in cases in which there are several layers of decorations). Pie dough that is thinner than that can tear or leak filling during the baking process. To determine whether my dough is the correct thickness, I use a trick I learned from the Epicurious website. Simply stack two quarters on top of each other: that's ⅛ inch (3 mm).

Lining a Pie Plate or Tin

Fitting dough to a pie plate or tin is quite a simple task once you've done it a few times. Here are some techniques for getting that floppy piece of dough from your work surface to the bottom of the pie plate or tart tin with finesse.

The Rolling Pin Method

The rolling pin method works best for transferring pie dough to deep dish and regular pie plates. Place your lightly floured rolling pin at the dough edge farthest away from you. Use your fingers to flip the edge of the pie dough up onto the pin, and then slowly roll the pin toward you with the dough loosely wrapped around it (photo A).

Before you lift the dough, make sure you have one or two fingers of each hand on the roller part of the pin to keep it from spinning and dumping your dough onto the counter or floor. Now, gently lift the rolling pin with the dough sheet on it and position it about ½ inch (13 mm) over the rim of the pie plate. Unfurl the dough from the rolling pin into the pie plate (photo B).

If you've miscalculated the center of the pie, you can gently readjust your pie dough, just be sure not to tug or stretch it.

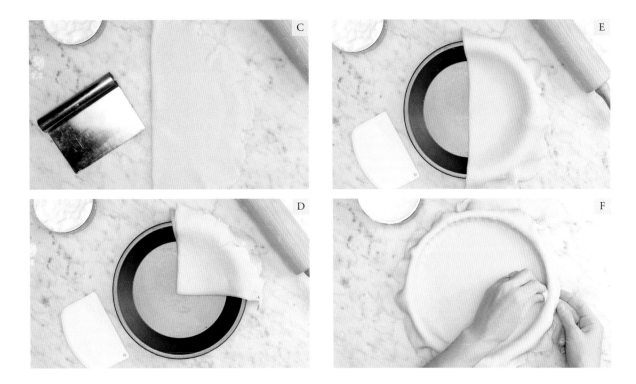

The Fold/Unfold Method

I use this method for transferring pie dough to tart tins to avoid having those sharp tart tin edges tear or cut through the pie dough. Use a bench scraper or your fingers to gently fold the rolled-out sheet of pie dough in half (photo C) and then half again. Once folded, gently transfer it to the top right quadrant of the tart tin (photo D) and unfold it once (photo E) and then again.

Fitting Pie Dough to the Pan or Tin

After you have transferred the pie dough to the plate or tin, use the pads of your fingers to gently fit the pie to the bottom and sides of the plate. If you are using a tart tin with a scalloped edge, cut a piece of dough from the excess overhang, dip it in a little flour and use it to push the dough into the tart tin crevices and corners (photo F).

Trim the overhang on both pies and tarts to 1 inch (3 cm) unless otherwise indicated in the recipe.

Tip:

Don't despair if your pie dough tears as you transfer it to the plate or tin. Because it won't be seen, you can simply patch it by dampening a finger with water and then dabbing it along the edges of the tear to moisten it. Sprinkle a little flour over the tear and use your fingers to gently press the rip back together again. If your pie top happens to tear, see if the rip or hole can be covered with a decoration. If that's not possible, it's best to reroll the top as the rip is likely to be even more obvious after the pie is baked.

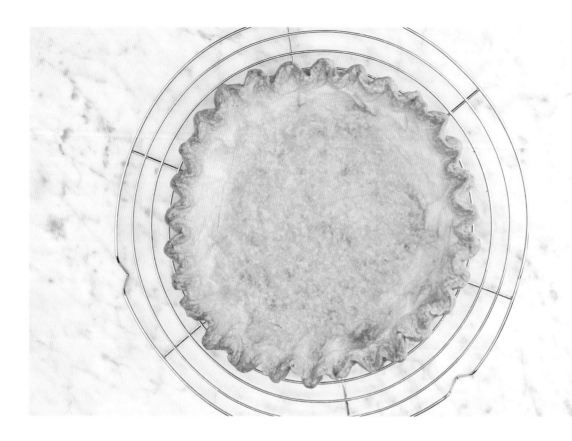

Partial and Full Blind Baking

Blind baking refers to prebaking the shell, without any filling, and then adding the filling after the shell is baked. Depending on the length of time that you have blind baked the shell, the pie may go back into the oven with filling to bake further (a partial blind bake) or it can be filled with cooked filling like a curd and left to cool (a full blind bake).

To blind bake a tart or pie shell, start by lining your tin or pan with pie dough, following the technique for Lining a Pie Plate or Tin on pages 170 and 171. If the pie edge is to be crimped or decorated, like the Summer Lemon Curd Fruit Wreath tart on pages 50 to 52, do this before you blind bake the shell, following the recipe's directions. If the edge is to be left plain, like the Mid-Century Modern Lemon Meringue Tart on pages 84 to 86, leave 1 inch (3 cm) of dough hanging over the edge of the tin (you'll trim it later), and reserve a small amount more to fix any holes or tears that might happen during baking. Place the shell in the refrigerator to chill for at least 15 minutes. While the shell is chilling, adjust the oven rack to the lower-middle position and place a baking sheet on it. Preheat the oven to 400°F (205°C).

After the pie shell has chilled, cut a piece of parchment paper about 2 inches (5 cm) wider than the tin or pan, scrunch it up into a ball and then smooth it back out. Fit the paper into the shell, being careful not to disturb the overhang or decorated edge (photo A).

Fill the parchment-lined shell with dry rice or beans, pushing them gently into the corners and edges of the pan or tin. These weights are what will keep your pie from slumping or shrinking in the pan, so take the time to ensure that they are firmly fitted against the edges of your shell.

Place the pie shell on the preheated baking sheet in the oven for 15 minutes. Remove the pie from the oven and, holding firmly onto both ends of the parchment, lift the parchment (with the pie weights) from the pie shell (photo B).

Using a fork, gently prick all over the bottom and sides of the pie to keep the dough from puffing up after you put it back in the oven.

For a partial blind bake, return the pie shell to the oven for 5 to 7 minutes, or until the shell is dry and lightly colored. For a full blind bake, return the pie shell to the oven and leave it for another 13 to 15 minutes, or until it is golden brown.

For both a full and partial blind bake, watch the shell carefully at this final stage. If the pie shell begins to puff up in the oven, use the tines of a fork to deflate it.

Remove the pie shell from the oven. If your shell already has a decorated edge, leave it to cool and then proceed with the recipe. If the tart has overhang, while the dough is still warm, use a sharp paring knife on an angle against the rim of the tart tin or plate to gently shave away any excess pie dough, giving a neat edge to your pie (photo C).

Tip:
To repair holes and tears that may happen during baking, use a small offset spatula to smear a small amount of uncooked pie dough across the hole/tear. For a full blind bake, place the tart back in the oven and bake for an additional 5 minutes to set the dough. For a partial blind bake, you can proceed with your recipe, as the dough will bake when the pie is returned to the oven.

Embossing Pie Dough

Embossing pie dough is one of my favorite ways to give a pie a custom look. You can emboss your dough with almost anything as long as it's clean and food safe. I've used cookie cutter impressions, doilies and table mats, but my favorite embossers are silicone or plastic impression mats. They are durable, make a nice deep impression and are easy to clean.

To make any type of impression on the dough, start by ensuring that your dough is well chilled. On a lightly floured surface, roll out the dough to a ¼-inch (6-mm) thickness (the embossing process will thin the dough further).

Place the impression mat on the dough surface. Using a rolling pin, roll over the mat once, applying enough pressure to leave a deep impression. Avoid rolling over the mat more than once as the mat may shift slightly, leaving you with an offset impression.

Depending on the size of your mat, you may need to reposition it if you are trying to cover the entire pie top. In this case, stop applying pressure just before you reach the end of the mat. Reposition the mat so it lines up with the impression you've already made, and make sure it faces the same direction as your previous impression. Continue making impressions this way until you have covered the dough.

Tip:

To ensure your impressions survive the baking process, freeze the pie for at least 1 hour before baking it. I like to leave my pies overnight in the freezer. Brush your impressions with additional egg wash before baking so that the egg wash pools in the impressions and stands out when baked.

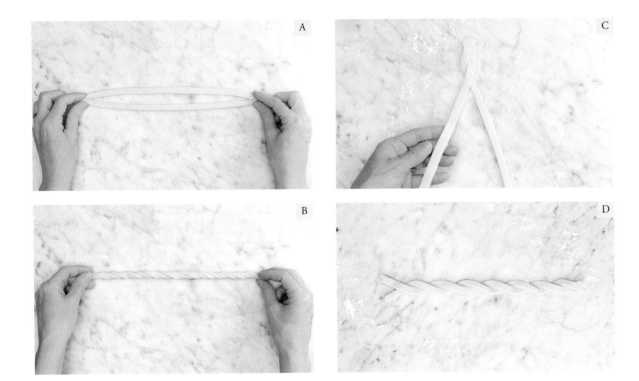

Twist and Braiding Techniques

There are several twists and braids used in the recipes in this book. Here's how to make them.

Twists

Lay two strips horizontally in front of you, about 1 inch (3 cm) apart. Pinch the strips together at both ends (photo A).

Gently twist the strips in opposite directions to give the strips a spiralled look. Gently press the ends to keep them in place so they don't untwist when you let go (photo B).

Two-Strand Braid

Lay two strands of dough side by side. Pinch the strands together at the top. Lift the right strand and cross it over the left strand (photo C).

The left strand is now your right strand. Repeat this process until you have braided the length of the dough strips (photo D). Leave the ends of the strands loose until you have laid the braid onto the pie, at which point you can trim them.

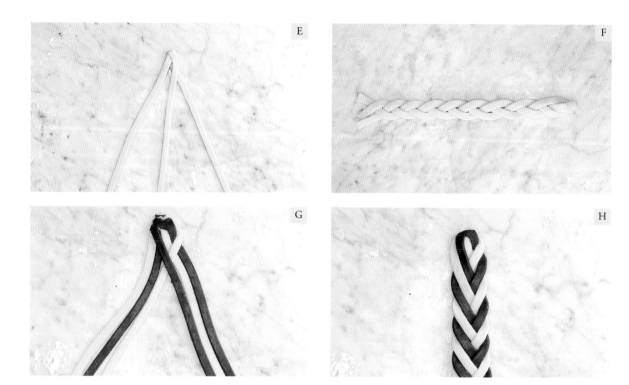

Three-Strand Braid

Lay three strands of dough side by side. Pinch the strands together at the top. Lift the right strand and cross it over the middle strand (photo E).

The right strand is now your middle strand. Lift the left strand and cross it over the middle strand. The left strand is now your middle strand. Repeat this process until you have braided the length of the dough strips (photo F). Leave the ends of the strands loose until you have laid the braid onto the pie, at which point you can trim them.

Six-Strand Braid

This technique can be used with a single color of dough, or with two colors to create a two-tone effect. The following instructions are for a two-tone braid. On a floured surface, side by side, alternate three strips of the two colors of dough, such as three strips of Everyday All-Butter Pie Dough (page 21) strips and three strips of Chocolate Pie Dough (page 21). Pinch the tops of the strips together. Divide the strips so there are three strips grouped on the left side, and three strips grouped on the right side.

Starting on the far right, lift the strip and cross it over two strips so that it now lays in the middle. Lift the dough strip on the farthest left and cross it over three strips so that it lays in the middle (photo G).

Repeat this process until you have braided the length of the dough strips (photo H). Leave the ends of the strands loose until you have laid the braid onto the pie, at which point you can trim them.

Latticing a Pie

Is there anything prettier than a latticed pie? I don't think so. Whenever possible, I like to lattice my pie tops on parchment paper, and then slide them onto the pie when complete. This allows me to move strips around without having to worry about staining them with filling or tearing them. The key to this technique is ensuring that you have properly chilled your finished lattice so it is easy to move.

The lattice shown here is a basic pattern that uses one disc of dough. A tighter lattice will use two discs. When you build up your confidence and skills, check out the many online resources there are for completing different types of weaves and lattice. Trust me, they are addictive.

To make a lattice for a 9-inch (23-cm) pie, lay out a piece of parchment paper. Turn your pie plate upside down and mark the diameter with a pencil or marker on the parchment. Set aside the marked parchment paper. On a lightly floured surface, roll out a disc of pie dough to a 12-inch (30-cm) circle. Using either a lattice cutter or a sharp knife and ruler, cut twelve ¾-inch (2-cm) strips of dough (photo A).

Turn the parchment over, ensuring that you can see the mark through the paper. Lay six strips, evenly spaced, across the circle. Use the longer strips for the center of your lattice and the shorter ones for the side (photo B).

Carefully fold back every other strip to just below the middle of the pie. Lay one strip across the folded back strips, taking care to be as straight as possible (photo C).

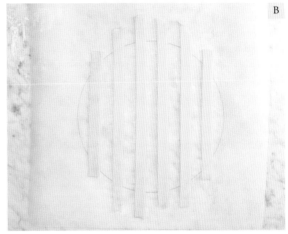

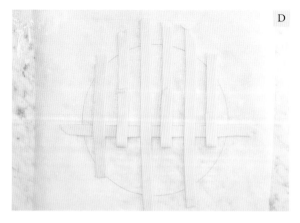

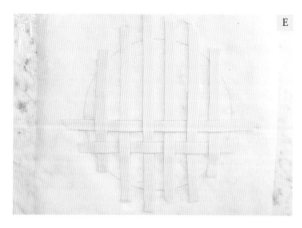

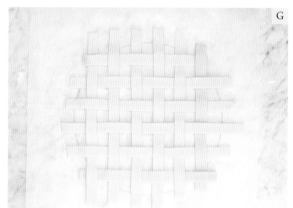

Fold the vertical strips back over the horizontal strip. Fold back the opposite set of vertical strips (the ones you did not fold back the first time) to approximately ¾ inch (2 cm) below the horizontal dough strip (photo D).

Lay another strip of dough across the pie. Fold the vertical strips back down over the horizontal strip (photo E).

Fold back the opposite set of vertical strips and lay in another horizontal strip. Fold the vertical strips back down over the horizontal strip. You should now have the bottom half of the pie latticed.

Rotate the parchment (photo F) and follow the same pattern for the other half of the pie lattice (photo G).

When you have used up all the strips, gently slide the parchment paper with the lattice design on it onto a baking sheet and place it in the freezer for at least 30 minutes. After your lattice is well chilled, it will be easy to simply slide it onto your pie top. When the lattice is in place on the pie top, let the dough warm up for about 5 minutes on the pie before you finish the edges.

Crimping a Pie Edge

A crisp, distinct crimp on a pie is a thing of beauty, and you'll be surprised by how easy it is to achieve.

Use a pie plate that has a substantial lip of at least ½ inch (13 mm) so you have somewhere to build your crimp. Then, check your overhang. I like to have at least 1 inch (3 cm) of overhang to build a substantial crimp and compensate for any shrinkage that might happen in the oven. Start by folding the overhanging dough under itself and pressing to seal the filling inside the pie if you are working with a pie top (photo A).

To crimp the pie, use the index finger of your dominant hand to press the inside edge of the pie dough outward while "hugging" the finger with the thumb and index finger of your nondominant hand (making a "V" shape) on the outer edge of the dough (photo B). For a larger crimp, use your thumb instead of the index finger of your dominant hand.

To make your crimp even more dramatic, use a trick I learned from baking genius Tessa Huff. After making your preliminary crimp, use the same technique but in reverse. Hook your dominant index finger in the inward facing crimp and "hug" it on the inside edge with the thumb and index finger of your nondominant hand (photo C).

Pull your hands away from each other to create a wavy, gorgeous crimp (photo D).

Sources

Amazon—Wide range of baking tools, silicone molds, impression mats
amazon.com

Ateco—Single and multiple lattice cutters, palette knives, turntables
atecousa.com

Baking Steel—Baking steels and accessories
bakingsteel.com

Cuisinart—Food processor
cuisinart.com

Escali—Digital weight scales
escali.com

Foxrun—Cutters and tart tins
foxrunbrands.com

Kirkland—Parchment paper
costco.com

Lee Valley—Embossing rolling pins
leevalley.com

KitchenAid—Mixer and accessories
kitchenaid.com

Michaels—Pie pans, tools, craft brushes and utility/ hobby knives
michaels.com

Mrs. Andersons—Silicone crust shield
hickitchen.com

Norpro—Silicone rolling mats
norprowebstore.com

PME—Plungers and cutters, bakeware, baking accessories
trade.pmecake.co.uk

Pyrex—Glass pie plates
pyrex.com

USA Pan—Metal pie plates
usapan.com

Whetstone—Rolling pins
whetstonewoodenware.com

Williams-Sonoma—Decorative cutters, tart tins
williams-sonoma.com

Acknowledgments

To my editors, Sarah Monroe and Caitlin Dow, thank you for being there to support and encourage me (and rein me in when required) and for helping me realize the vision I had for this book. To my line editor, Simone Payment, thank you for your attention to detail and for hanging in with me as I worked to get it right.

To Kylie Alexander, thank you for the stunning layout and design. I know it was no small task, but you did a beautiful job bringing this cookbook to life.

To Rebecca Firth, Janet Piper and Nina McCreath, for sharing their experiences about the publishing world. The time you took to share your insight and wisdom was greatly appreciated.

To my amazing manuscript reviewers and recipe testers, Fiona, Olivia and Sheena. The care and attention you put into reading through hundreds of pages and testing these recipes was invaluable. I can't thank you enough.

To my team of taste testers, Sean, Karen, Jim, Liam, Carl, Fiona and Sheena. It was a tough job but someone had to do it! Thank you so much for your honesty and enthusiasm (and I'm sorry about those extra pounds).

To Karen, thank you for all the amazing props and your unvarnished advice and opinions. I wouldn't have it any other way.

To my mother, for getting the ball rolling by teaching me to bake in the first place and for always being my biggest cheerleader. You will always be my baking idol.

To my father, who supported everything I did always. I hope you're watching and that I've made you proud.

To my boys, Devlin and Liam. Thank you for being such enthusiastic eaters and for your constant love and support. I love you.

To Millie, our mini Schnauzer, who sacrificed many long walks because I was too busy in the kitchen. I promise to make it up to you with a double river walk soon.

Finally, and most importantly, to Jim. We did it! Thank you for the beautiful photography in this book and for all your love and support. To say I couldn't have done it without you would be an understatement. Your patience, humor and unwavering faith in me kept me going on the bad days and made the good days even sweeter. So, what's next?

About the Author

Helen Nugent is a self-taught baker. What started out as a way to share her pies with friends and family took on a life of its own through her Instagram feed, @batterednbaked, collaborations with the Food Network and pie-making workshops. Called the creator of "Instagram's Most Stunning Pie Crusts" by *Better Homes and Gardens* magazine, Helen's work has been featured on the Food Network, in *Taste* magazine and Canada's national newspaper, the *Globe and Mail*. Her pies have also been seen on numerous social media accounts including Town and Country, Williams-Sonoma, Better Homes and Gardens and Bake from Scratch.

She lives with her family in Toronto, Canada.

Index